YOU CAN TEACH YOURSELF ®

DOBRO ®

by Janet Davis

GW00569923

AUDIO CONTENTS

1. Tuning (1:05)
2. Rhythm 1 (:27)
3. Rhythm 2 (:38)
4. Finding the Melody (1:11)
5. Goodnight Ladies (:50)
6. Basic Forward Roll (:17)
7. Basic Roll Patterns (1:25)
8. Lesson 4 (:42)
9. Chord Progression (:23)
10. G Chord Licks (:48)
11. Salty Dog (:26)
12. Salty Dog (Slow) (:35)
13. G Lick #1 (:15)
14. G Lick #2 (:18)
15. Wabash Cannonball (:42)
16. Wabash Cannonball with Guitar (:27)
17. G Lick #3 (:35)
18. Cripple Creek (:28)
19. Cripple Creek (Slow) (:34)
20. Cripple Creek (Alternate Rhythm) (:23)
21. Lick #1 (:23)
22. John Hardy (:31)
23. John Hardy with Guitar (:23)
24. Blackberry Blossom (:49)
25. Blackberry Blossom (Slow) (:55)

26. Closed Chord Lick #2 (:31)
27. Home in Dixie (:46)
28. Home in Dixie (Slow) (:44)
29. C Arpeggio (:14)
30. G Lick #4 (:12)
31. Footprints in the Snow (:23)
32. Footprints in the Snow (Slow) (:40)
33. The Glissando (:14)
34. Great Speckled Bird (1:10)
35. Dark Hollow (:37)
36. Dark Hollow (Slow) (:31)
37. Wabash Cannonball (One String) (:31)
38. Licks #5, #6, #7 (:26)
39. Wabash Cannonball (:36)
40. The Vibrato (:18)
41. John Henry (:37)
42. Chord Progression #1 (:57)
43. G Lick #7 (:20)
44. Chord Progression #2 (2:06)
45. The "Foggy Mountain" Lick (:48)
46. Train 45 (1:39)
47. D Lick #1 (:21)
48. Sunnyvale Breakdown (1:29)
49. Interchanging Licks (:43)
50. Train 45 (1:08)

51. D Lick #4, Grandfather's Clock (2:42)
52. Interchanging D Licks (:35)
53. Hamilton County Breakdown (1:51)
54. Substitute for Part B (:28)
55. Seventh Chords (:34)
56. Other Alternate for Part B (:35)
57. Closed Lick #4 (:23)
58. John Hardy (1:27)
59. Train 45 (1:08)
60. D Lick, Reuben (1:10)
61. Salt River (1:42)
62. She'll Be Comin' Around the Mountain (:42)
63. Rolls and Licks (:38)
64. Lonesome Road Blues (:27)
65. Roll Patterns and Licks (:20)
66. Roll in My Sweet Baby's Arms (:26)
67. The Choke (:33)
68. John Hardy (1:40)
69. G Major Scale (:14)
70. Sally Goodin' (2:01)
71. Fisher's Hornpipe (1:03)
72. G Scale Exercise (:54)
73. Bill Cheatham (:47)
74. Melodic Style (:21)

75. Flop Eared Mule (1:56)
76. Single String Technique (:28)
77. Devil's Dream (:59)
78. The F Scale (:17)
79. Red Haired Boy (:48)
80. The Modal Sound (:24)
81. Old Joe Clark (1:27)
82. Minor Chords (:15)
83. Greensleeves (:48)
84. The Battle of Jericho (:29)
85. House of the Rising Sun (:47)
86. Amazing Grace (Melody) (:17)
87. Amazing Grace (:35)
88. The Tremolo (:21)
89. Silent Night (1:03)
90. Silent Night (Ver. 2) (1:01)
91. In the Pines (:47)
92. In the Pines (Ver. 2) (:30)
93. Sailing to Hawaii (1:15)
94. When You and I Were Young, Maggie (1:08)
95. Silver Threads Among the Gold (1:15)
96. Dixie (1:44)
97. Aloha Oe (1:30)
98. Will There Be Any Stars? (:45)

Online Audio & Video

Audio
www.melbay.com/95227EB
Video
dv.melbay.com/95227
You Tube
www.melbay.com/95227V

1 2 3 4 5 6 7 8 9 0

Visit us on the Web at www.melbay.com — E-mail us at email@melbay.com

MEL BAY ®

Table of Contents

History of the Resophonic Guitar

The Resophonic Guitar was developed by five of the Dopera brothers in the mid 1920's. Technically, this instrument is a forerunner of the electric guitar and electric pedal steel guitar. The principle behind the original instrument involved using three resonator cones to amplify the sound from the guitar. Although the first guitars were of metal bodies, the Dopera Brothers offered these as either wood bodied or metal bodied instruments in the 1930's. They also offered a choice of the amplified guitar with a round neck, or an amplified lap-style guitar with a square neck, where the strings were raised high above the frets, so that a steel slide could be used with the left hand when playing, without the strings touching the fretboard. The lap-style, square neck model is the one with which this book will be concerned. (It is also referred to as a resonator guitar, lap steel, Hawaiian steel, DOBRO®, hounddog, etc.)

During World War II, the Dopera brothers stopped making these instruments, for it was illegal to use the metal necessary to build them at this time. Electric instruments became the fashion after the war, especially by the 1950's. However, the uniqueness of the resophonic guitar could not be duplicated and it continued to be in demand by those who knew and loved its sound. In the 1960's, Ed Dopera formed the Original Musical Instrument Co. (OMI), and again began production of the original resophonic guitar. He also began offering a resophonic banjo, mandolin, and other instruments. Although Ed Dopera passed away in 1976, the OMI company continued producing these guitars until the mid 1990's, when the Gibson Guitar Corporation purchased the company.

The term, DOBRO®, was first registered as a trademark which belonged to the Original Music Company, founded by the Dopera Brothers. However, through time, the term "DOBRO®" has often been used to refer to the instrument itself, regardless of the manufacturer. In the 1990's, Gibson Guitar Corporation purchased the OMI Company along with the trademark. Therefore, the term, DOBRO®, is now registered to The Gibson Guitar Corporation.

Although the resophonic guitar was originally developed during an era when Hawaiian music was popular, it soon became an integral part of a variety of bands playing different types of music. Many people associate this instrument with old-time country music and western swing. For example, Jimmy Rodgers used resophonic guitar players such as Cliff Carlisle in his recordings. The resophonic guitar is also associated with the music of Merle Haggard (with Norman Hamlett playing the resophonic guitar), Bob Wills (Leon McAuliffe), Roy Acuff (Brother Oswald- Pete Kirby), Shot Jackson, Hank Williams (Don Helms), and many others. Even Maybelle Carter played the resophonic guitar. The resophonic guitar has provided the background music for many movies. It has also become a great blues instrument through recordings of Babe Turner, Oscar Wodds, Bill Weldon and others. Bluegrass musicians such as Josh (Buck) Graves with Flatt & Scruggs, Mike Auldridge who has recorded with the Country Gentlemen, the Seldom Scene and others, and Jerry Douglas who has recorded with too many artists to name, have made the resophonic guitar a standard in bluegrass music.

The main purpose of this book is to provide you with the techniques which you can use to play and enjoy any and all types of music on the resophonic guitar.

It's Fun!

The resophonic guitar is not only unusual and fascinating to most audiences, but it is also fun to play. It has a beautiful tone, and can be used to play many types of music. Once you begin, you will find that, surprisingly, it is not that difficult to learn, and no previous musical knowledge is needed. I have taught people of all ages, young and old, and they all have a good time pickin' and grinnin'.

This book is presented in lesson format. I recommend working progressively from the first lesson through the last lesson, in order. This book will cover several of the most popular styles used for playing the DOBRO® e.g. Bluegrass-style, oldtime country, blues, Hawaiian, fiddle tunes, and more. Remember, however, that they all use the same basic playing techniques and the same chord positions; the basic principles will apply to anything you play.

It is helpful to realize that the left hand is working with chord positions, even though these are produced with a steel bar, rather than with the fingers. The same chords are used for many different songs. Open strings will often be used for the G chord because the DOBRO® is tuned to a G chord. Also, using the bar to slide from one position to another is a very integral part of the "sound" of the DOBRO®. In many cases the steel bar, rather than the right hand, will sound the tones. Usually you will slide only one or two frets, when moving into a chord position. Remember, you are sliding to a note *and* from a note. Both pitches are important. Randomly hitting a fret to slide from, may defeat the purpose of the slide.

As you work through the lessons in this book, you will find that there are two primary ways to handle the bar when playing songs on this instrument:

1.) One method is to hold the bar across the strings to form chords. Generally, in this style, the right hand will pick two or more strings simultaneously, as the left hand slides the bar to another chord position. 2.) The other method is to tilt the bar to play single notes. The bar will only touch one string at a time. It is important to realize that although different songs may favor one method over the other, most songs will use a combination of these barring techniques.

NOTES: _____

*1.) The Resophonic Guitar is often generically referred to as a "DOBRO®."

2.) When playing the resophonic guitar, it is important to place the metal bar on the strings, *directly over* the fret bars, not between them, as you would with a guitar or other fretted instrument.

3.) On this instrument, you do not have to play as many notes as on a banjo, fiddle and/or mandolin to be effective. The notes are often sustained for a longer duration on the resophonic guitar.

4.) The left ring & pinky fingers rest on the strings, behind the bar.

5.) The above will make more sense as you work through each lesson.

The Resophonic Guitar

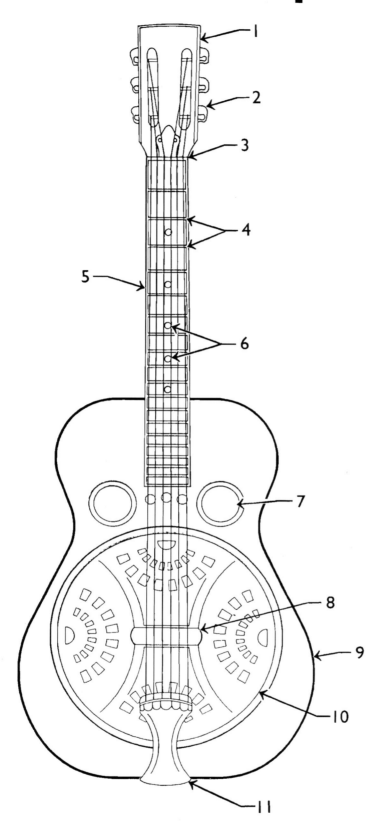

PARTS OF THE GUITAR

1. PEGHEAD
2. TUNING KEYS
3. NUT (higher than on Spanish style guitar)
4. FRETS
5. NECK
6. INLAY POSITION MARKERS
7. SOUND HOLES (covered by screens)
8. BRIDGE
9. BODY
10. RESONATOR COVER PLATE
11. TAIL PIECE

• Lesson 1 •
Tuning

G Tuning

The standard tuning used for the resophonic guitar is called "G Tuning" or "universal tuning." The strings are tuned to a G chord. This instrument can be tuned to itself *without* using another instrument. Lay the resophonic guitar flat in your lap:

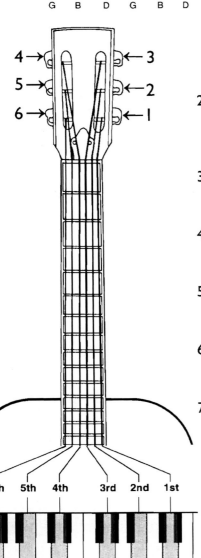

1.) The strings are numbered in order:
   The 6th string is the string closest to your body; it is tuned to the deepest pitch (G).
   The fifth string is next to the sixth string (B).
   The fourth string is next to the fifth (D).
   The third string is next to the fourth (G).
   The second string is next (B).
   The first string is furthest from your body (D).

2.) To tune, start with the sixth string. This string is the deepest tone of all the strings. It is normally tuned to a **G**, (the second G below middle C on the piano). All of the other strings will be tuned in relation to this string.

3.) Tilt the steel, and touch the sixth string directly over the 4th fret; tune the fifth string to this pitch (**B**). The open fifth string sounds like the sixth string at the 4th fret.

4.) Note the fifth string with the bar at the 3rd fret and tune the fourth string to this pitch (**D**). The open fourth string sounds like the fifth string fretted at the 3rd fret.

5.) Note the fourth string at the 5th fret, and tune the third string to this pitch (**G**). The open third string sounds like the fourth string fretted at the 5th fret.

6.) Note the third string on the 4th fret and tune the open second string to this pitch (**B**). The open second string sounds like the third string fretted at the 4th fret.

7.) Note the second string on the 3rd fret and tune the open first string to this pitch (**D next to middle C**).

When tuned correctly, the strings will sound a G chord when strummed. **Also:** The 1st & 4th strings will sound in unison, an octave apart (D's); the 2nd & 5th strings should sound alike (B's); the 3rd & 6th strings should sound alike, an octave apart (G's).

NOTES: _____

1.) A piano or a pitch pipe will help. Electronic tuners are also available which are easy to use and automatically tell you when each string is in tune.

2.) HINT: If a string is out of tune and you can't tell if it is too high or too low...loosen the string first, then tune it. This way you will know it is low, and you can tighten it until it is in tune. (And you won't break the string by going tooooo high.)

3.) The steel bar should depress the string precisely over the metal fret bar.

• Lesson IA •
Holding the Resophonic Guitar

Looking good is the first step to sounding good!! (Even if you don't know what you are doing, a lot of people will think you do.)

Have a good time, and your listeners will, too!
Relax, but...

Sit up straight if you are seated. Stand up straight if you are standing.

Lay the guitar flat on your lap, if you are seated.

To play standing up, a strap (preferably all leather) will aid in holding the guitar securely.

THE STRAP: NOTICE that the strap is under the shoulder and over the forearm!

*This is the standard way to wear a strap. However, when right hand harmonics are used in later lessons, you must pull the right hand out from under the strap.

The *left hand* touches the steel bar to the strings, directly over the metal fret bars, to produce the tones.

The *right hand* should rest on the metal bridge on the resonator for support when picking the strings.

• Lesson 1B •
The Right Hand

Only three fingers are used to pick the strings of the Resophonic Guitar:
The *Thumb, Index* (first) finger, and the *Middle* finger.

Your hand should be relaxed.

You will need three picks:
A plastic thumbpick
Two metal fingerpicks

Thumbpick (plastic)
The point should aim toward the floor into the guitar—
not up in the air.
The curve should be around the fingernail side of the thumb.
The straight side is on the flesh side of the thumb.

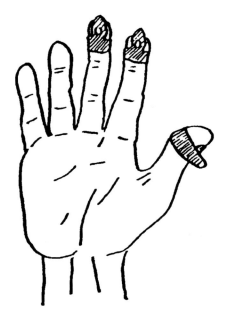

Fingerpicks (metal):
Wear one on your index (first) finger and
one on your middle finger (of your right hand.)
Wear the curved part along the flesh side of your finger,
not the fingernail side!

Bend the picks to fit snugly.

The picks should extend about ⅛" from the tips of your fingers.
(Experiment for comfort, clean picking and tone.)

Place the picks on your fingers so they pick the strings on the flat side...
(If at an angle, they may squeak on the strings.)

Picks are a personal choice (experiment).
Most professionals use a fairly stiff thumbpick (plastic). Often a thumbpick doesn't fit. Reshape it by holding it in hot water, then molding it. It should fit tightly enough so that it doesn't slip.

The metal fingerpicks may feel awkward at first. However, eventually you will probably prefer them. The heavier gauged metal picks provide more tone from your DOBRO®. Bend your picks, if necessary, to get the best tone. A short extension from the end of your finger may make playing easier. A longer extension provides a crisper tone. Wrapping the fingerpick flush around the tip of the finger results in more picking power.

• Lesson 1C •
Picking The Resophonic Guitar

Right-Hand Picking:

Pick the strings with three fingers only.
The thumb plucks away from your body.
The two fingers (index & middle) pluck toward your body.

The Right Hand Position:

Right-hand placement is very important.
Rest your hand across the metal bridge over the strings.
Rest your pinky (and ring) on the metal resonator.

NOTE: You can vary the right hand placement later, to produce different tone qualities from your instrument. However, this is the standard position.

At first you may want to watch your right hand, in order to pick the correct strings. Try to avoid watching this hand as time goes on, or it may slow down your playing.

It is better to watch your left hand than your right hand. It is better yet to look at your audience. Make it look EASY.

NOTES:_____

1.) Pick with short strokes.

2.) T = Thumb; I = Index; M = Middle.

Move off the bridge to vary the tone.

• Lesson 1D •
The "Steel" Bar

When playing the resophonic guitar, the left hand touches a metal bar to the strings, directly over the metal frets on the fingerboard, to produce the tones. Several different types of bars, usually referred to as "the steel" or "slide," can be used to play the resophonic guitar. These are generally made of chrome-plated brass or steel. The Steven's Steel is probably the most preferred among bluegrass players. The Shubb/Pearse bar is a variation of the Steven's steel with a longer nose. Shubb/Pearse also makes a shorter #2 model, which is becoming quite popular. Dunlop makes a round tonebar, which is often preferred by pedal steel guitarists who play this instrument.

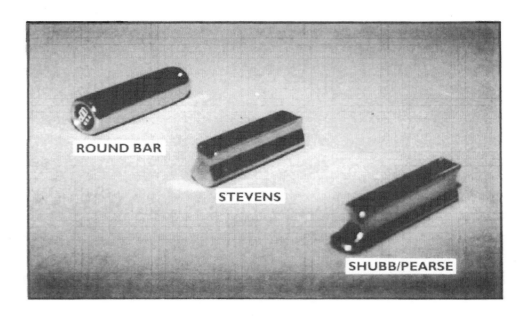

• Lesson IE •
Holding the "Steel"

Holding the steel bar will be explained using the Steven's steel and the Shubb/Pearse bar. However, the same procedure can be adapted to the round bar, (& other types), even though it does not have the indention for the index finger.

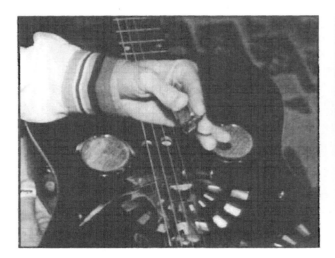 

The left hand should hold the bar in a relaxed manner, but firmly enough to control it:

1.) Place your left index finger in the groove along the top of the bar.

2.) Place your left middle finger in the groove along left side of the bar, and your thumb in the groove along the right side of the bar.

3.) Your ring and pinky fingers should rest *on the strings* behind the bar, (the nut side of the fingerboard). As you slide the bar, these fingers will slide upon the strings. (These two fingers will develop calluses.) When you lift the bar to move to a new position, these two fingers should be the last to leave the strings. Roll them off, with the bar leaving the strings first. This helps dampen unwanted tones, and stops the tones from running into one another.

4.) Your wrist should be loose and relaxed.

5.) When playing, the steel should be placed directly over the metal frets on the fingerboard— not between them.

NOTES: _____

1.) *You will have to train your left ring and pinky fingers to stay on the strings — they will want to float in the air.

2.) The index finger determines the amount of pressure that is applied to the strings. A fairly firm, but light touch will produce a clear tone.

3.) The middle finger may extend past the bar, which is fine. It can also be used to dampen unwanted tones.

11

• Lesson 1F •
Chords and Single Notes

Playing Suggestions:

1.) A firm, but relaxed touch will produce a solid tone. However, do not try to depress the string to the fingerboard. The strings should not touch the fingerboard.

2.) REMEMBER to keep your *left* ring & pinky fingers *on the strings* behind the bar.

3.) LIFT THE BAR completely off of the strings to move to a different chord position, unless the slide is indicated.

4.) When playing songs, you will *either* be holding *chord positions* with the steel bar across several strings at one time, or you will be noting *single notes* by tilting the bar to "fret" only one string at a time.

BARRE CHORD POSITION
Place the Stevens bar
directly over the fret bar,
across all six strings.

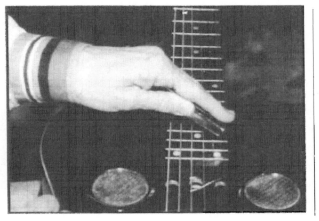

SINGLE NOTE TECHNIQUE
Tilt the bar & touch the tip of the bar
to one string only.

Playing Chords:

The "barre" or "straight" chord position is the most common way to play a chord. The left hand will hold the steel bar straight across the strings, directly over the metal fret bar, (not in between the bars). Any chord can be played in this position, depending upon which fret number the bar is covering. See diagram (next lesson). The bar can be placed over all 6 strings, or only over a few of the strings, depending upon what you are playing. (See the beginning of *Salty Dog* for an example.)

Picking Single Notes:

Tilt the bar, touching only the tip end of it to one string, directly over the fret bar, in order to play one note at a time. This is a commonly used technique in this book. Remember to keep the ring and pinky fingers on the strings in back of the bar. *Sunnyvale Breakdown* uses this technique throughout.

NOTES: _____

    1.) With the use of the above techniques, you should have no trouble learning each of the songs in this book.

Slant Chord Positions:

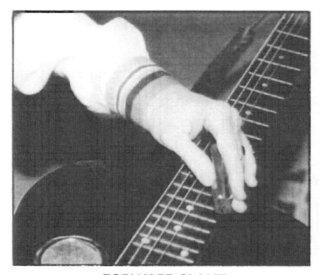

FORWARD SLANT
Place your index finger to the
side of the bar.

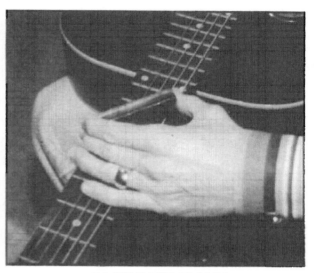

BACKWARD SLANT
Hold bar with thumb & middle finger;
index holds onto top front.

Forward Slant:

A standard slant chord involves *angling* the bar so that it covers *different* frets to form the chord. To play a slant chord, turn the bar so that it covers the first two or three strings, but over a different fret number for each string. Move your index finger to the side of the bar, off of the top, when playing slant chords. This will help you to smoothly switch from the straight position to a slant position, without having to awkwardly move your wrist. Slant chords may take some practice, in order to quickly achieve the correct intonation from the chord.

Backward Slant:

The Backward Slant is the most difficult of the chord positions to master. However, with practice, it too will become easy. Hold your left thumb against one end of the bar and your left middle finger against the other end. The index finger helps control the bar by holding onto the top front edge still in the groove (Steven's Steel).

NOTE:
1.) Slant positions will be covered in detail later in the book.

13

• Lesson 1G •
Tablature

Tablature is a simple system designed for those who do not read music. It can be learned in a few minutes. Basically, it is comprised of lines, numbers, and stems.

The six lines are the six strings of your Resophonic Guitar. Each line represents a particular string.

The numbers are fret numbers; these tell you which fret to cover with the steel bar on a particular string. To begin playing, place the "steel" across all six strings over the designated fret number; however, pick only the string indicated (with the number on it).

For example: A number on the 3rd line from the top means to play the 3rd string. If the number is a "2," place the bar over the 2nd fret and pick this string; if the number is a "4," place the bar over the 4th fret before picking the string. A "0" means to pick the string open (without using the bar).

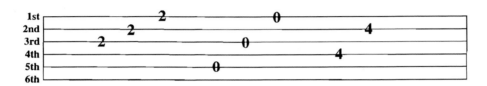

Summary:

• The lines tell you which string to pick; the number(s) tells you which fret number(s) to depress (on that string) with the steel bar.

• The *lines* are the six strings of your Resophonic Guitar:

• The *numbers* are *fret numbers:* **4**

• Two numbers, one over the other, $\frac{0}{3}$, are to be played at the same time.

• On the DOBRO®, the following combinations are commonly picked simultaneously:

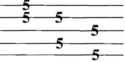

1st & 2nd strings;
2nd & 4th strings;
3rd & 5th strings.

Notice that only the 1st & 2nd are adjacent strings. The other combinations are separated by a string.

• **Picking Fingers** (Right hand):
T=Thumb; I=Index; M=Middle
(Only three fingers pick the strings.)

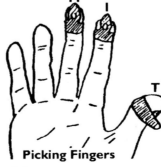

14

Rhythm

The **duration,** or length of time each note should *ring,* is indicated by the **stem,** or line which is drawn from each number. This is referred to as the **rhythm** or **timing.** Accurate timing is very important when playing the Resophonic Guitar.

♪ The **eighth note** is a common unit in music for the Resophonic Guitar.

There will be eight eighth notes in one measure of tablature. Each eighth note should receive equal duration. **Do not hold one eighth note longer than another.**

Two measures of eighth notes should be picked evenly, without stopping between the measures:

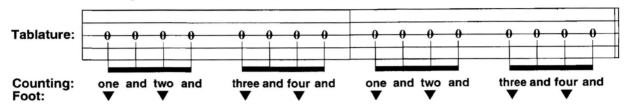

Tablature:

Counting: one and two and   three and four and   one and two and   three and four and
Foot: ▼ ▼   ▼ ▼   ▼ ▼   ▼ ▼

♩ The **quarter note** is also a basic unit in music for the Resophonic Guitar.
The quarter note is held (should ring) twice as long as an eighth note.   ♩ = ♫
(Two eighth notes must be played in the same amount of time one quarter note is held.)

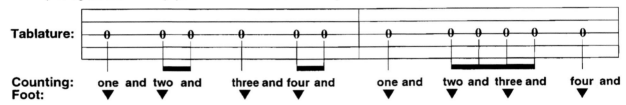

Tablature:

Counting: one and two and   three and four and   one and   two and three and   four and
Foot: ▼ ▼   ▼ ▼   ▼   ▼ ▼   ▼

2→3 A **stemless** note followed by an arrow + a note means to slide quickly to the 2nd note.

♬ Play two **sixteenth** notes for the duration of one eighth note.   ♬ = ♪

♩ ♪ **Syncopated rhythm:** hold the quarter note twice as long as the eighth note following it. (long-short)

♩. A **dotted note** is held 1½ times the normal value of the note.   ♩. = ♩ + ♪

✗ An **X** in your tablature means to **sustain the previous note** for the duration determined by the stem beneath the X. Pick the note, then let it ring for the duration of the X (i.e. quarter) notes. (Do not pick the string for the "X".)

Rests = silence for the indicated duration.

𝄽 A **quarter rest** means to stop the sound for the duration of 1 quarter note.

𝄾 An **eighth rest** means do *not* play for the duration of an eighth note (½ beat).

𝅝 A **note with no stem;** hold (sustain) this tone for the entire measure (4 beats).

♩♩♩ A **triplet;** play three notes in the same amount of time you normally play two eighth notes,
 3 or one quarter note (1 beat). (Accent the 1st note of the triplet.)

LEFTHAND (Steel Bar)
INDICATIONS:

NOTE: The lessons which follow will demonstrate each of these techniques in depth.
These explanations are primarily to be used as a reference.
The following indications will appear beneath or in some cases above certain notes in your tablature.

sl   under a number means to *slide* the bar to this fret from the previous fret. This note is to be sounded by the slide (left-hand) *only*.

sl   means to slide the steel to this fret from the previous note, *then pick* the string with the
T   Thumb of the right hand.

12→10 both notes are picked with the right hand, but the bar should slide from the first fret number
T T   (12) to the second (10).

H   **Hammer:** sound the note by hitting (hammering on) the string with the tip of the steel (tilt the bar).

P   **Pull-Off:** sound the open string by plucking the string with the bar. You will pick the note occurring just before the "P," *then* pull the bar off of the string. The bar should literally pluck the string to sound the open tone.

CH↑   **Choke:** Pick the note indicated, then bend the string to raise the pitch.

CH↓   **Choke:** Bend the string before picking it, then pick it, then straighten the string to lower the pitch.

X   sustain the previous tone through this beat, without picking the string again.

∿∿   **Vibrato:** helps sustain the tone by oscillating, or moving the bar back and forth over the fret, as if you had tremors. Some people go as far as ½ fret either direction, but take care not to get too far out of the accurate pitch for the tone. The rate of the vibrato is up to you...experiment. (This is the same technique vocalists use with their vocal cords.)

Tr   **Tremolo:** alternately picking two different strings, rapidly: (Both the vibrato and tremolo work well with the triplet as the rhythmic basis – playing 3 notes for each beat.)

⌢   **Legato:** play the phrase smoothly and connected, without lifting the bar.
♪ ♪

.   **Staccato:** sharp, quick tone; dampen the string with your left (ring) finger immediately after
♪   picking the string with the right hand.

2⌢4   quick slide to the (second) note, after picking the first note.
|
sl

16

Additional Tablature Symbols:

||: :||

Repeat sign. Play this section again, before going to the next section. Return to the previous repeat sign if there is one, otherwise, return to the beginning of the song and repeat the entire section.

|1. |2.

1st ending & 2nd ending. Play the song through the measures in the 1st ending; then, return to the beginning; repeat the entire section but the second time, omit the first ending, and substitute the measures belonging to the 2nd ending, instead. (Continue with the song if there is more following these endings.)

NOTES: _____

1.) These symbols are a form of musical shorthand which are used when a section of a song is to be repeated. If there are only repeat signs, repeat the same part exactly. If there is a first and second ending, play the first ending the first time and the second ending (only) the second time.

17

Natural Harmonics (chimes):

NOTE: Harmonics will be covered in depth in later lessons. The following is intended as a reference.

Harmonics are the bell-like tones which are often used in slower songs, in Hawaiian-style songs, and to produce the effect of church bells or chimes in a variety of songs. These are fairly simple to play, and produce a beautiful tone from the DOBRO®. There are two types of harmonics:

Natural Harmonics, are produced without using the steel bar and can be played over only certain frets on the fingerboard:

Natural Harmonics:

These tones are produced by lightly touching the string(s) with the outside edge of the palm or little finger of your left hand across certain fret numbers. To produce this effect, lightly touch the side of your left hand to the strings over the 12th fret bar. Pick one string with your right Thumb, then quickly lift your left hand to let the tone ring.

Natural harmonics can be produced only over certain frets. Harmonics are commonly produced at the 12th fret, 7th fret, and 5th fret. (These divide the string in ½, ⅓, & ¼ respectively.)

NOTE:_____

Natural Harmonics are caused by dividing the string in exact fractional parts. You can also produce harmonics at the 24th, 19th frets. (Notice that if you pick all of the strings over one fret, you can produce the G chord at the 5th, 12th & 24th frets, and a D chord at the 7th & 19th frets. Harmonics can be played at the 4th, 9th and 16th frets to produce the B chord, but they are more difficult to produce clearly. The 17th also produces a G chord, and the 22nd fret produces an F chord.

Artificial Harmonics:

Artificial Harmonics:

This type of harmonic is more versatile for it can produce virtually any desired tone in harmonic form. This type of harmonic uses the steel bar with the left hand, and can be played over any fret. Because artificial harmonics can be produced from any fret number, they can be used to produce any tone as a chime.

There are two common ways to produce artificial harmonics:

      1.) PALM HARMONICS, which use the edge of the palm of your right hand to produce the harmonic;

      2.) FINGER HARMONICS, which use the right middle or ring finger to cause the harmonic.

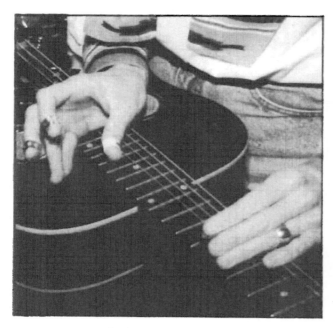

PALM HARMONICS

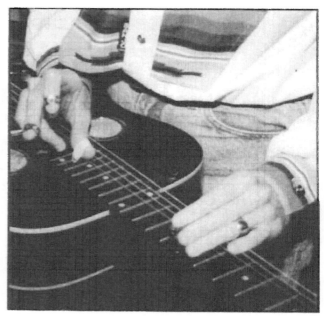

FINGER HARMONICS

Palm Harmonics: Place the bar in a standard chord position; touch the strings precisely 12 frets away from the bar with the edge of your *right hand*. Use your right thumb to pick the string, then quickly lift your right hand to allow the tone to ring. This may take practice, but is widely used on the DOBRO®... especially in back-up.

NOTE: It doesn't matter where the right thumb picks the string.

Finger Harmonics: If you only need to play the harmonics on one string, you can use your *right ring finger* to stop, or note, the string 12 frets from the bar, instead of the side of your entire hand. Pick the string with your right thumb, then release the ring finger to hear the chime.

• Lesson 2 •
Chord Locations

It is important to learn the location of the chords — notice that they move up the fingerboard *alphabetically*. Up means *higher* in fret number — toward the resonator. The musical alphabet has only 7 letters (A through G) which are repeated. (After G, start with A again — there is no "H".) Notice that several chords have two names, (i.e. A# & Bb). Although you can use either name for the chord, technically, when moving up the scale line, the sharp (#) name is used and when moving "down" the scale line, for example, from B to Bb, the flat name is used.

Each of the following chords is to be played with the standard bar position. Place the steel bar directly over the metal fretbar across all six strings for each chord.

HINT: If you are just beginning to play the Resophonic Guitar, *learn* the locations of the **G** chord (open & 12th fret), the **C** chord (5th & 17th frets), and the **D** chord (7th & 19th frets). You will use these chords in virtually every song you play.

G	G#/Ab	A	A#/Bb	B	C	C#/Db	D	D#/Eb	E	F	F#/Gb	G
0	1	2	3	4	5	6	7	8	9	10	11	12
0	1	2	3	4	5	6	7	8	9	10	11	12
0	1	2	3	4	5	6	7	8	9	10	11	12
0	1	2	3	4	5	6	7	8	9	10	11	12
0	1	2	3	4	5	6	7	8	9	10	11	12
0	1	2	3	4	5	6	7	8	9	10	11	12

G	G#/Ab	A	A#/Bb	B	C	C#/Db	D	D#/Eb	E	F	F#/Gb	G
12	13	14	15	16	17	18	19	20	21	22	23	24
12	13	14	15	16	17	18	19	20	21	22	23	24
12	13	14	15	16	17	18	19	20	21	22	23	24
12	13	14	15	16	17	18	19	20	21	22	23	24
12	13	14	15	16	17	18	19	20	21	22	23	24
12	13	14	15	16	17	18	19	20	21	22	23	24

• Lesson 2A •
Finding The Melody
Within The Chord Positions

The melody or tune for a song consists of the notes you would sing for the song. A common way to find the melody notes for a song to be played on the DOBRO® is to look within the chord positions for these specific notes. Generally the melody notes can be found either within the chord positions, or somewhere close by on the fingerboard.

For example, play through *Wabash Cannonball:*
Notice that when the song calls for the G chord, the melody notes are:

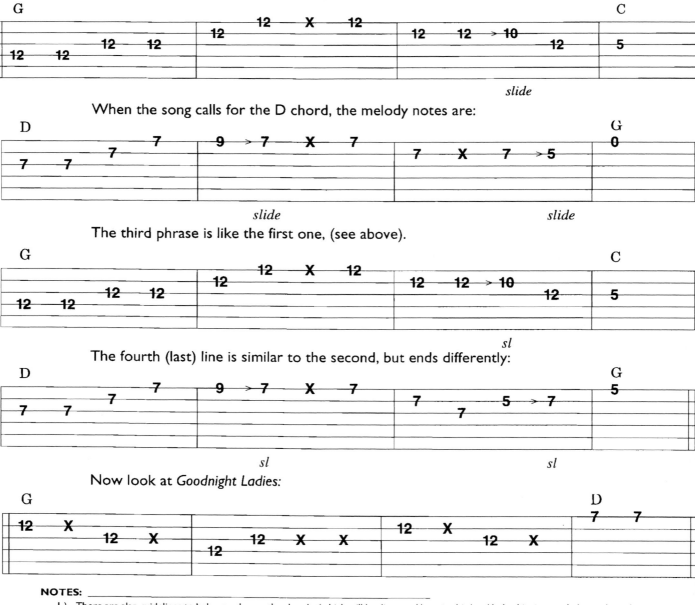

When the song calls for the D chord, the melody notes are:

The third phrase is like the first one, (see above).

The fourth (last) line is similar to the second, but ends differently:

Now look at *Goodnight Ladies:*

NOTES: _____

1.) There are also guidelines to help you choose the chords, (which will be discussed later in this book). At this time, to help you learn by ear, remember the recommendation in the "Chord Locations" pages: "learn the G, C, & D chords." Notice that these chords are used in both of these songs, and will be present in many of the songs in this book. Written music will often provide you with the chords.

Goodnight Ladies

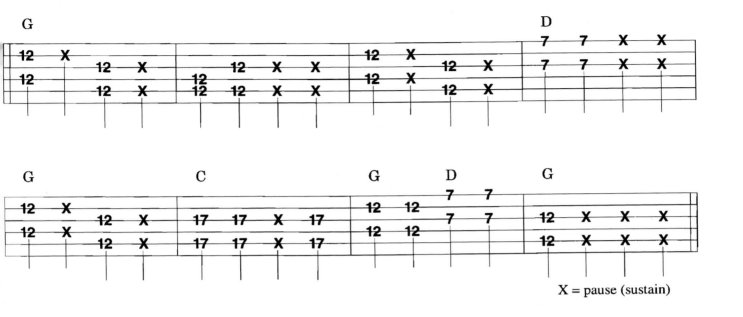

X = pause (sustain)

Variation
Adding Slides

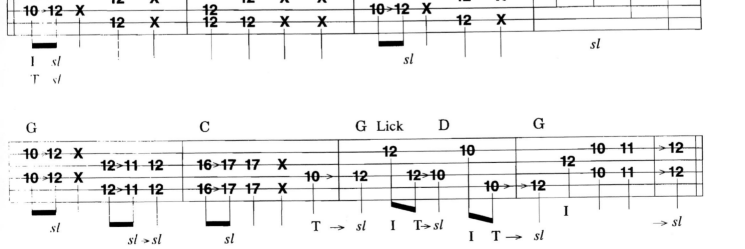

• Lesson 3 •
Roll Patterns

Roll patterns provide the basis for songs which are played in the bluegrass-style on the Resophonic Guitar. Each roll pattern is a right hand fingering pattern which can be played with any chord. *There are only four basic roll patterns to learn.* These patterns can be used in many different songs. Often, these patterns are used in songs to add a surge of energy to the music.

Definition: A roll pattern is a right-hand fingering (picking) pattern. The order or sequence in which the right-hand fingers follow one another when they pick the strings determines the name of each pattern.

For Example: **The forward roll = T I M T I M T I** (notice the fingering order or pattern.):

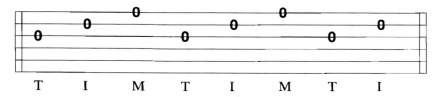

T I M T I M T I

Thumb - Index - Middle - Thumb - Index - Middle - Thumb - Index

Actually, this pattern can begin with any finger, but the picking sequence must remain the same — e.g. thumb follows middle finger.

Each pattern consists of eight eighth notes (one measure of music or tablature).

*Each roll pattern can be played while holding *any chord* with the left hand. (However, each of the roll-pattern examples on the following page is written using only open strings. No left-hand action is required to learn the patterns.)*

You can also practice these patterns on a table or on the steering wheel when you are driving.

NOTES: _____

1.) Generally, the rolls are used to add drive and/or interest to the music, without actually changing the tempo.

2.) Roll patterns will make more sense as you progress through the book. However, I strongly recommend practicing each of these patterns right from the beginning. They will increase your dexterity, and you will have a better understanding of their use when you start working with songs which include the rolls.

The Basic Roll Patterns

1. Forward Roll (T I M T I M T I)

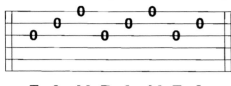

T   I   M   T   I   M   T   I

Variation (different strings)

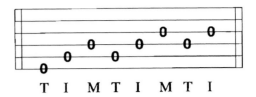

T   I   M   T   I   M   T   I

2. Backward Roll (M I T M I T M I)

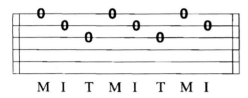

M   I   T   M   I   T   M   I

Variation (different strings)

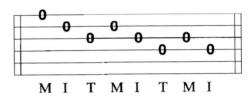

M   I   T   M   I   T   M   I

3. Forward-Reverse Roll (T I M T M I T M)

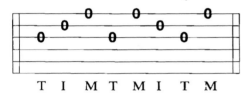

T   I   M   T   M   I   T   M

Variation

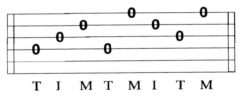

T   I   M   T   M   I   T   M

4. Mixed Roll or Alternating Thumb Roll

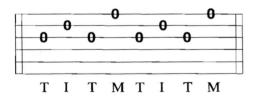

T   I   T   M   T   I   T   M

Variation

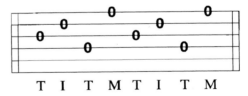

T   I   T   M   T   I   T   M

NOTES: _____

1.) With the forward roll, you may have a tendency to play nine notes, including an extra note. Each roll pattern has only eight notes.

2.) At the end of the pattern, you can begin the same pattern again, or you can play a different pattern. Do not stop between patterns—keep your rhythm smooth and steady.

3.) Learn the name of each pattern. (Notice right-hand fingering.)

4.) With experience, you will learn to recognize these patterns upon hearing them.

5.) *Use these patterns as warm-up exercises.*

• Lesson 4 •
Licks – Picking Patterns

In addition to playing the basic tune for a song, Resophonic Guitar players often use certain recurring patterns, which can be played for virtually any song. Once you have played the instrument for a while, you will begin to develop a vocabulary of *licks* or *picking patterns* which you can use in many different songs. In other words, the *same* "licks" can be used to play different tunes. There are two categories of licks:

I. Licks which can be played for any chord:

Many licks are *fingerboard patterns* which can be played for any chord. Simply place the bar in the proper location on the fingerboard for the desired chord, then follow the fingerboard pattern. For example:

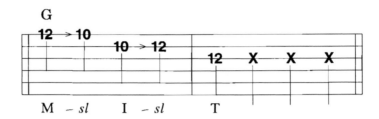

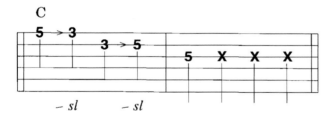

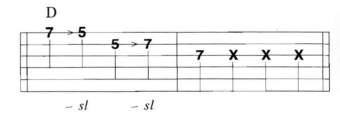

To play this "lick":
1.) place the bar across all six strings at the 12th fret (for the G chord);
   pick the 1st string with your right middle finger;
2.) then slide the bar to the 10th fret to sound the 2nd note; (do not pick this note with your right finger).
3.) next, pick the 3rd note while the bar is at the 10th fret;
4.) then slide back to the 12th fret to sound the 4th note, (do not pick with right hand);
5.) now pick the last note in the pattern.

NOTE:_____
   1.) Licks will be presented throughout this book in specific lessons.

25

The following chord progression is used for many songs:

G = 12th fret; C = 5th fret; D = 7th fret.

Learn the locations for these three chords; they will be used for many, many songs. The example below demonstrates using only the above lick pattern for each chord.

CHORD PROGRESSION
Using One Lick Pattern

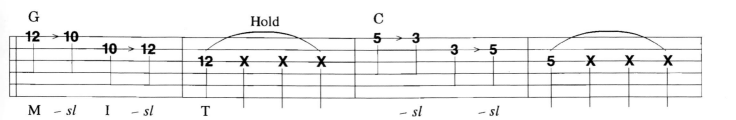

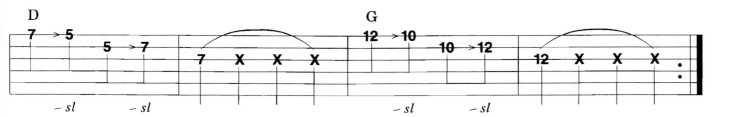

```
NOTE:

    X   means to sustain or hold the note for 1 beat. (Let the note ring.)

    ⸲   A rest means to stop or silence the tone for 1 beat.
```

NOTES:

1.) Remember: *sl* under a note means that note is sounded only by the slide—do not pick with the right hand.

2.) Remember to keep your left ring & pinky fingers on the strings behind the bar.

3.) Do not lift the bar from the strings until you change to a new chord.

4.) Remember that the X's and rests are as important to good timing as the notes; each X above equals a quarter note...sustain the tone through each X for the duration of a quarter note.

II. Licks which can be played only for certain chords.

The following licks are played only for the G chord. Tilt the steel bar to "fret" or note only one string for each note with the tip of the steel. (Do not lay the bar across all of the strings.) Each lick can be played in any song when a G chord occurs. These licks are interchangeable.

G CHORD LICKS
Licks that can be played *only* for the G chord.

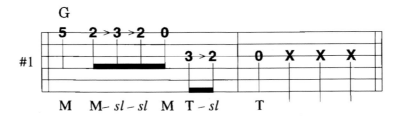

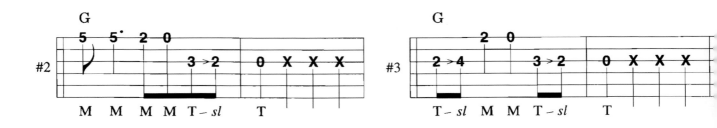

For Practice: Substitute Lick #1 (above) for the G chord at the end of the *chord progression* on the previous page.

NOTES: _____

1.) Notice the G chord at the end of each song in the following lessons. Try to become aware of licks and the chords for which they are used as you work through the arrangements. The more of these patterns you know, the sooner you will be able to improvise.

2.) As you progress through the lessons in this book, you will add one lick at a time to your vocabulary, which will also be used in subsequent songs. There are many standard licks which can be played for each chord. Learning these one at a time will enable you to easily build a lick vocabulary from which to work out your own arrangements.

• Lesson 5 •
Playing A Song
"Salty Dog"

The following procedure below should help you learn to play any song on the Resophonic Guitar. In this lesson, these steps will be demonstrated with the well known bluegrass tune, *Salty Dog*.

1.) Learn the positions for the chords which are used to play the song.

The following are the chords for *Salty Dog*. (You will slide the steel in and out of these fretboard positions when playing the actual arrangement for the song.)

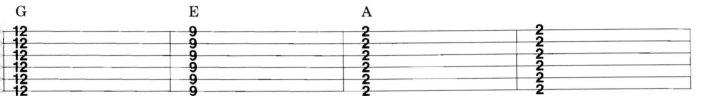

2.) Look for fingerboard patterns.

In *Salty Dog*, notice that the same pattern is used for the G chord and the E chord. (Notice that the A chord (m. 3) had two fast slides.)

3.) Remember to play slowly and steadily, in order to play the correct timing.

In *Salty Dog*, play one note for each beat in mm. 1 and 2. Be sure you pause or rest for the 4th "beat." (Allow 1 beat of silence for the rest.)*

4.) Work through the song by sections, (i.e. 4 measures at a time).

In *Salty Dog*:
1.) Play through the first three measures, plus the 1st note of the 4th measure. (This is like a line of poetry.)
2.) Next work on the 2nd phrase or sentence, beginning with the last two beats of m. 4, as pick-up notes into this last phrase.
3.) Learn the lick, (last two measures of *Salty Dog*), after you have comfortably worked through the first portion. Work on the lick alone, as an exercise, then put it with the song.

NOTE: _____

1.) REST = silence; the duration of the silence is indicated by the type of rest:

𝄽 = quarter rest (silence for 1 beat)

𝄾 = eighth rest (silence for ½ beat – the same duration as an eighth note is to ring.)

Salty Dog

Key of G

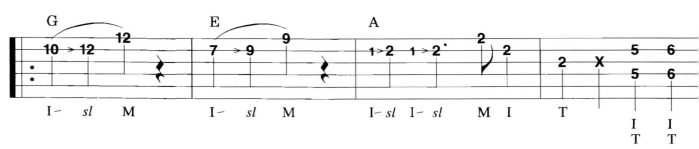

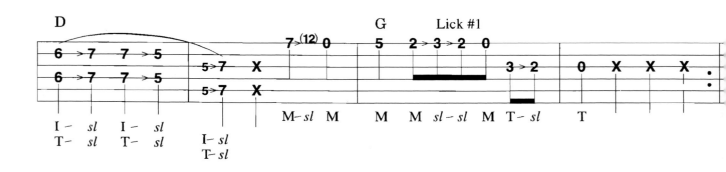

NOTE: → *sl* means to *slide* the bar to the note;
Do not pick this note with the right hand!

NOTE: ⌢ means the music should sound connected.
Do not lift the bar from the strings while playing these notes.

X = PAUSE (Sustain the previous note for the X.)

Helpful Hints for "Salty Dog"

1.) Hold the steel straight across all six strings for every measure, (except the last two measures, which play the G "lick").
Pick *only* the strings indicated by the tablature with the right hand.

2.) *sl* means to *slide* the bar to this note.
Do not pick the string to sound this tone.

3.) *Lift the steel* from the strings to move to each new chord location.
i.e. Lift the steel to move to the 7th fret (D chord) in the 2nd measure.
Remember to lift the ring and pinky fingers last.

4.) $7 \rightarrow {}^{12}0$ = means to pick the string, then slide the steel up to around the 12 fret; next: lift the steel, then pick the open string.
(Tilt the steel to fret only the 1st string at the 7th fret.)

5.) The final two measures (G chord) consist of a "lick." This pattern can be played (substituted) in any song for the final G chord.
Tilt or angle the steel to "fret" only the string indicated by the tablature.
Do not hold the bar across all six strings.

G LICK #1:

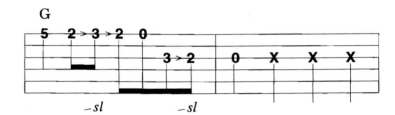

To play the G Lick (7th measure):

1.) Tilt the steel to fret only the 1st string, 5th fret; pick the 1st string with the right middle finger.

2.) Lift the steel and move to the 2nd fret; pick the string with the middle finger.

3.) Next, slide the bar to the 3rd fret, then back to the 2nd fret. Do not pick the string for these notes. They are sounded only by the slide.

4.) Lift the steel; pick the open 1st string.

5.) Tilt the bar and fret the 3rd string at the 3rd fret.
The steel should touch only the 3rd string.

6.) Slide the steel to the 2nd fret.

7.) Pick the open 3rd string.

8.) ‖: :‖ = repeat sign; play through this entire arrangement twice. This equals one complete arrangement ("break") for *Salty Dog*.

NOTE: _____

1.) Remember to place the steel bar directly over the metal fret bar when chording or noting single notes.

• Lesson 6 •
The Hammer
"Wabash Cannonball"

In addition to the *slide*, several other techniques can be used to produce tones on the resophonic guitar with the steel by the left-hand. One of these is the *hammer*. The *"hammer"* is commonly used to add drive or a surge of energy to the music.

To **"hammer"** means to sound the tone with the steel bar by "hammering-on" the string at the appropriate fret number, instead of by picking the string.

The **hammer** is indicated by an **"H"** under the note in the tablature. It *always* follows a note played with an *open* string.

1. Pick the open 2nd string.

2. Next, tilting the bar, hammer-on this string over the 1st fret. (Hit the string over the 1st fret bar with the steel to sound the note — then hold it to sustain the tone.)

Important: you are sounding two tones — the tone before the hammer (the open string), and the tone played with the bar by hammering.

Double Stops:

When two notes appear together, one on top of the other in the tablature, they are to be picked (pinched) together, at the same time. One note will belong to the tune for the song, (the melody note), and the other note will harmonize with that tone. Notice as you work through this book, that double stops are not always played on adjacent strings. Frequently, the two notes are separated by a string.

G Lick #2:

The following lick is played at the end of *Wabash Cannonball* for the final G chord. (You can also play G Lick #1 from *Salty Dog* instead of this lick. These G Licks are interchangeable. The more G Licks you learn, the easier it will be to improvise.)

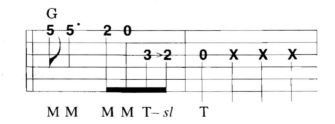

NOTES: _____

1.) See page 14 for commonly played double-stops. See page 27 for G licks #1, #2, & #3.

2.) Notice in *Wabash Cannonball*, that mm. 1-6 and mm. 9-14 are alike.
When you can play the first two lines, you will actually know almost the entire song.

Wabash Cannonball

Key of G

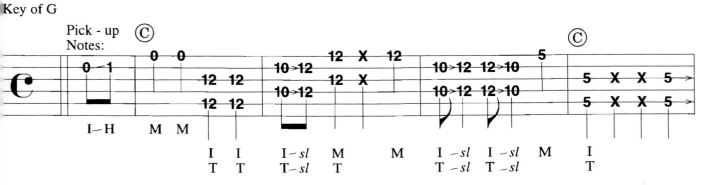

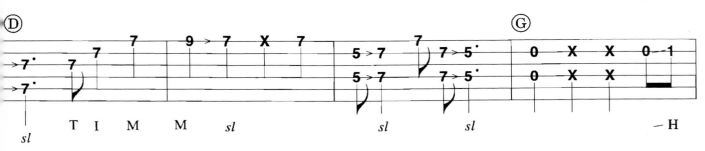

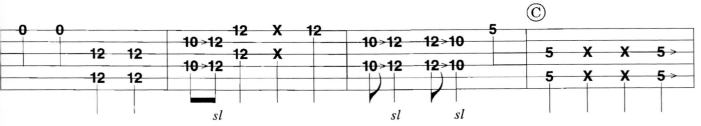

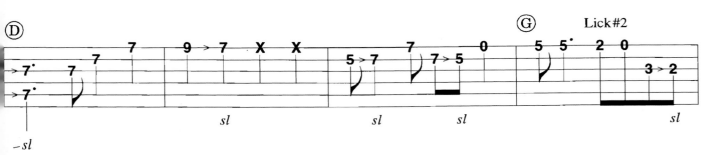

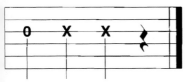

NOTE: H means **HAMMER**
Place bar on fret number to sound the tone with the Bar.
Don't pick this note with the right hand!

NOTE: **X** and 𝄽 both mean to pause — don't play for this beat.
However, for the **X**: sustain the previous tone;
for the 𝄽: stop the tone from ringing (w/left ring).

32

• Lesson 7 •
The Pull-Off
"Cripple Creek"

The *Pull-off* is a commonly used left-hand bar technique, which, like the hammer, helps add drive, and/or a surge of energy to your playing.

Pull-off means that an open string is sounded with the bar, by plucking the string with the tip of the bar, instead of picking it with the right hand.

This note has a **"P"** written under it in the tablature:

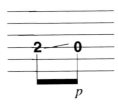

1.) *Tilt* the bar to touch only the 4th string at the 2nd fret.

2.) *Pick* the note just *before* the one with the "P" underneath. (Place the bar at the 2nd fret of the 4th string, then pick the string with your right Thumb.)

3.) Next, *pull-off* of the indicated fret (2), with the bar, to sound the open string. (Pluck the 4th string from the 2nd fret with the tip of the steel bar.) Do not pick *this* note (open string) with your right hand.

G Lick #3

The last two measures of Part A and the last two measures of Part B of *Cripple Creek* involve playing a "G" lick. Notice that the same lick is used to end each of these sections. This lick can also be substituted for the final G chord in *Salty Dog*, pg. 29.

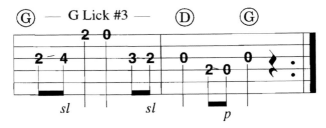

Many licks will involve tilting the bar, and will be played only for a specific chord.* Learn to apply each lick according to the *main* chord for which it is used.

NOTE: _____

1.) The above lick can be played for 2 measures of a G chord, as well as for one measure of a G chord followed by one measure of the D chord at the end of a section of a song. (Several G & D chord licks are interchangeable because they both contain the D tone.)

Cripple Creek

Key of G

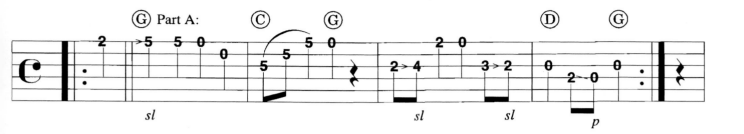

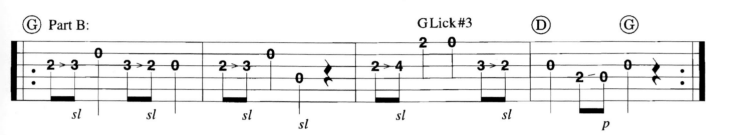

*Alternate Rhythm

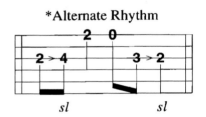

NOTE: **P** means to pluck this tone with the bar — (pull off the string).
This sounds the tone.

NOTE: Tilt the bar to note each tone, except 2nd measure (C chord).
NOTE: Learn Part A first; then work on Part B.
NOTE: The last two measures of each part are identical.
NOTE: Notice the repeat sign at the end of each section:
Play Part A twice; *then* play Part B twice.

• Lesson 8 •
Licks in Closed Chord Positions
"John Hardy"

This lesson demonstrates the use of licks which work from *chord positions*. These licks are fingerboard patterns which can be played for any chord, depending upon where the bar is placed. (Closed chord position licks belong to the category of licks which are played from chord positions and do not use the open strings.) In the following tab for *John Hardy*, the first line establishes the melody. After the first four measures, the arrangement consists primarily of licks which are played for the indicated chord. However, because of the first line plus the chord progression, the listener can easily identify this song as *John Hardy*, a well-known folk and bluegrass tune.

1.) Notice in measures 5 - 8, that the same lick is played for both the C chord and for the G chord. The fingerboard pattern for this lick begins from the barre position for the chord for which it is being played. (This lick was discussed earlier in this book, p. 25.)

**CLOSED
LICK #1:**

Closed
Lick #1:

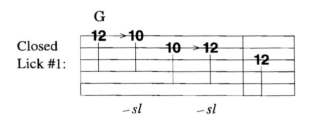 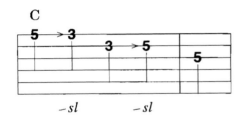

2.) Now, look at *John Hardy*; notice how many times this lick was used:

    1.) For the C Chord: line 2 (mm. 5 & 6 of the song);
    2.) For the C Chord: line 3 (mm. 9 & 10)
    3.) For the G Chord: line 2 (mm. 7 & 8)
    4.) For the G Chord: line 3 (mm. 11 & 12)
    5.) For the D Chord: line 4 (mm. 13 & 14)
    6.) For the D Chord: line 4 (mm. 15 & 16) {Notice m. 16}
    7.) For the D Chord: line 5 (m. 17) = rhythmic variation

John Hardy

• Lesson 9 •
Using Roll Patterns
"Blackberry Blossom"

Blackberry Blossom is a fiddle tune which is popular among resophonic guitar players. It is divided into two parts, which is a common feature of many fiddle tunes. Learn each part separately (as you did with *Cripple Creek*), then put it together. Remember to repeat Part A (play it twice) before playing Part B (also played twice).

Part A: *Notice that each measure of Part A plays a roll pattern.*

Measure 1 uses the Forward-Reverse Roll: T I M T M I T M.
Measure 2 uses a variation of the Backward Roll: M I T M I T M I.
Measures 3 & 4 use the Forward Roll: T I M T I M T I.
(Learn the name of each of the roll patterns as you practice. These patterns make good warm-up exercises.)

Each measure contains two different chords (involving two different positions on the fingerboard). Notice in the first measure that you move to the 7th fret after the first three notes. The right hand should not break the rhythm of the roll pattern when you move the bar. (Lift the bar off the strings to move to each new chord position, unless a slide is indicated in the tablature.)

Notice in Part A:

1st measure: A *slide* is used to move from the D chord to the C chord (7th to 5th fret);
2nd measure: a *pull-off* drives the music to the open G chord.
3rd measure: Place the bar across the 5th fret over all of the strings, *except the 1st string*.
  (Leave the first string open to play this measure.)
5th-7th measures: The last four measures are like the first four, except for the last measure.
Repeat Part A. Then play part B twice.

Part B: Tilt the bar to play all of the fretted notes except in measure 4 (B chord).
  Part B begins with the E minor chord, which includes open strings.
  (You can't brush across all six strings, when playing this chord.)

Notice in Part B:

a.) measures 1, 3, and 5 are basically alike;
b.) measures 1 & 2 are exactly like mm. 5 and 6;
c.) measure 4 calls for a B chord (across 4th fret).
  (Slide into the B chord from the 2nd fret.)

Exercise: Play through all of the chords in Part A as block chords:
  Pinch the first three strings for each chord.

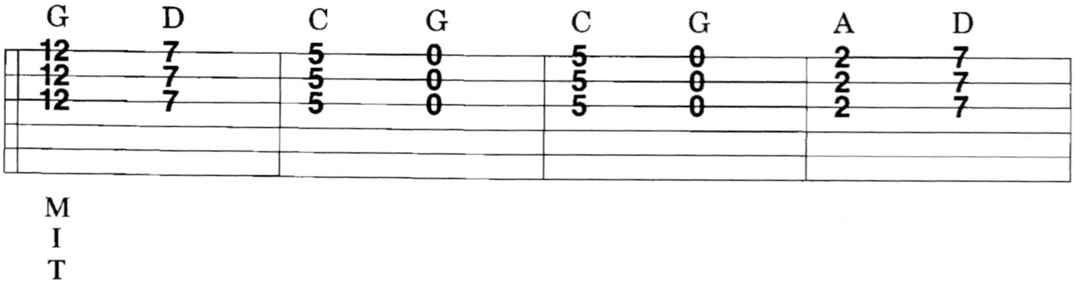

G	D	C	G	C	G	A	D
12	7	5	0	5	0	2	7
12	7	5	0	5	0	2	7
12	7	5	0	5	0	2	7

M
I
T

37

Blackberry Blossom

Key of G

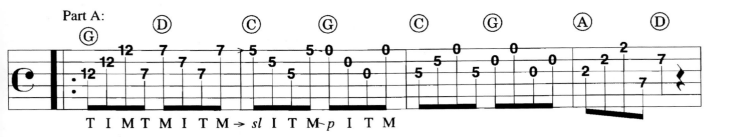

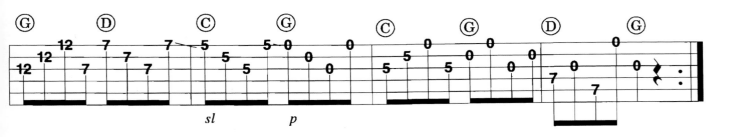

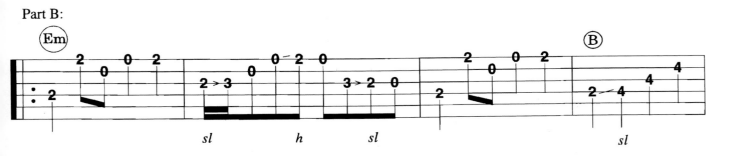

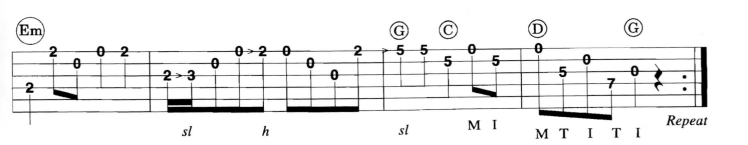

• Lesson 10 •
Understanding Rhythm
For Review

Rhythm is really quite simple. The quarter note ($^0_|$)sets the basic beat for the song. The beat is the pulse rate, or heartbeat of the song. If you played along with your heartbeat, using only quarter notes, you would play one note with each beat of your heart. If your heart beats slowly, your song would be slower, but you would still play one note on each beat.

The stems on the notes tell you how long a particular note is to be held through the beats. (e.g. $^0_|$ = hold the note for 1 beat, $^0_|$ $^X_|$ = 2 beats, or play two notes for 1 beat = $^0_|$ $^0_|$, etc.) There is a corresponding *rest* for each type of note; silence should "be played" for the correct duration of the rest. (i.e. a quarter rest = 1 beat of silence; an eighth rest = ½ beat of silence.)

In the songs you have learned so far, notice that the notes add up to four beats in every measure. In 4/4 time, the note values in each measure must add up to four. (Pick-up notes are only partial measures; they count as the last portion of the measure.)

For Review:

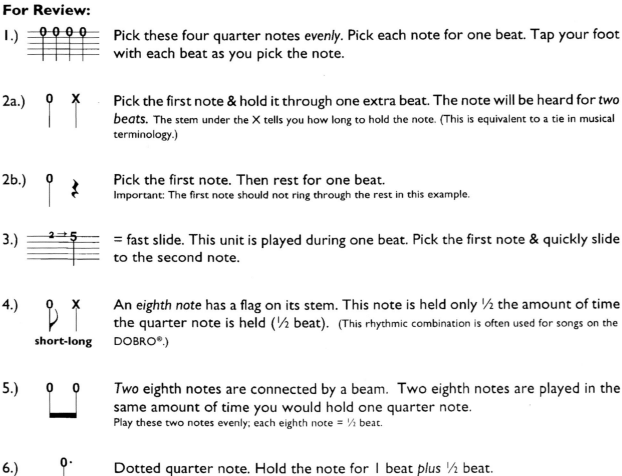

1.) Pick these four quarter notes *evenly*. Pick each note for one beat. Tap your foot with each beat as you pick the note.

2a.) Pick the first note & hold it through one extra beat. The note will be heard for *two beats*. The stem under the X tells you how long to hold the note. (This is equivalent to a tie in musical terminology.)

2b.) Pick the first note. Then rest for one beat.
Important: The first note should not ring through the rest in this example.

3.) = fast slide. This unit is played during one beat. Pick the first note & quickly slide to the second note.

4.) An *eighth note* has a flag on its stem. This note is held only ½ the amount of time the quarter note is held (½ beat). (This rhythmic combination is often used for songs on the DOBRO®.)
short-long

5.) *Two* eighth notes are connected by a beam. Two eighth notes are played in the same amount of time you would hold one quarter note.
Play these two notes evenly; each eighth note = ½ beat.

6.) Dotted quarter note. Hold the note for 1 beat *plus* ½ beat.

NOTES: _____

1.) Hold the notes followed by an "X" through the correct number of beats...do not cut these measures short, or your timing will be off.

• Lesson 11 •
1st and 2nd Endings
"Home in Dixie"

Notice at the end of Part A in the following song, that the tablature has a marking which indicates a 1st ending and a 2nd ending (over measures 7 - 9). This is a common shortcut used in music to avoid rewriting an entire section of a song when it is to be repeated, but ends differently each time it is played. The following symbol is used in conjunction with a repeat sign, and means to play the 1st ending the first time you play through the section, but to skip the 1st ending and play the 2nd ending, instead, when you repeat the section.

In other words, when you find this symbol in your tablature:

1.) Play Part A including the 1st ending (up to the repeat sign);
2.) Next, repeat Part A, but this time, substitute the 2nd ending; do not play the 1st ending when repeating Part A.
3.) Continue with the rest of the song.

CLOSED CHORD LICK #2:

A new closed chord lick is introduced at the end of the song. Remember, a closed chord lick pattern can be used for any chord. The lick below is often used for the final chord to end a song. (It will be played for the chord named for the key of the song. i.e. C chord for Key of C.)

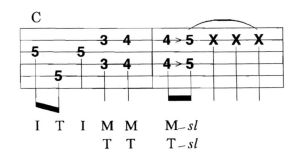
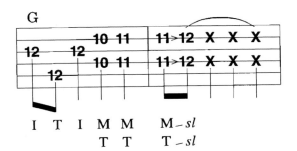

THE KEY OF C: C - F - G CHORDS

The following arrangement for *Home In Dixie* is played in the Key of C. Songs which are played in the Key of C usually use the C, F, and G chords. When a song is played in this key, the melody is often found from the chord positions (rather than using the open strings).

NOTE: _____

1.) *Home In Dixie* is played in the THE KEY OF C. The chords for this song are C, F, and G. Notice that the last chord is the C chord. The final chord of a song will usually tell you in which key the song is being played.

Home In Dixie

• Lesson 12 •
Up-The-Neck
"Footprints in the Snow"

Footprints In the Snow uses a very effective technique for looking good as well as sounding good. Notice that the 1st measure plays the C chord at the 5th fret, but the 2nd measure plays it at the 17th. When the melody notes move higher than those in the basic chord position, move to the same chord, 12 frets higher, to find the notes.

The higher fret numbers should not seem so ominous once you realize that the fingerboard repeats itself after the 11th fret. Beginning with the 12th fret, the chords start over again as you move the steel bar up the fingerboard, fret by fret.

If you use your 12th fret as a guide, (G chord), equating it with the open G chord, you should be able to locate any other barred chord located higher on the fingerboard, i.e. the C chord is located 5 frets up (in pitch or fret number) from the open G chord. The C chord is also 5 frets (the same distance) from the G chord at the 12th fret, (12 + 5 = 17th fret). Seven frets up from the 12th fret, and you have a D chord at the (19th fret).

Notice in the following exercise, that the notes sound smooth and tonally connected, as you pinch each successive double-stop.*

C
```
                    5           17
              5          17
         5       5  17        17
    5       5            17
5                   17
5
```

G Lick #4: For the G chord, tilt the steel bar to play each note, and hammer or slide where indicated. The first two measures are actually a *G Lick*. However, unlike the G Licks in *Salty Dog* and *Cripple Creek*, this lick imparts the feeling that something is about to happen, rather than functioning as a closing lick.

1.) Notice that the G chord uses the hammer to run up the scale line:

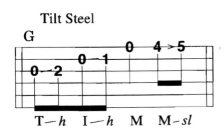

Tilt Steel
G

T—h   I—h   M   M–sl

This tune is played in the Key of C, which means that it uses the C, F, and G chords.
(The F chord is located across the 10th fret.)

NOTES: _____

1.) This is also called an arpeggio. Practice playing the arpeggio for the G chord by moving from the open strings to the 12th fret, and for the D chord (7th — 19th). Eventually, you should be able to connect the two positions for all of the major chords.

2.) See pages 20 and 133 for barre chord chart.

Footprints in the Snow

Key of C

Arranged by Janet Davis

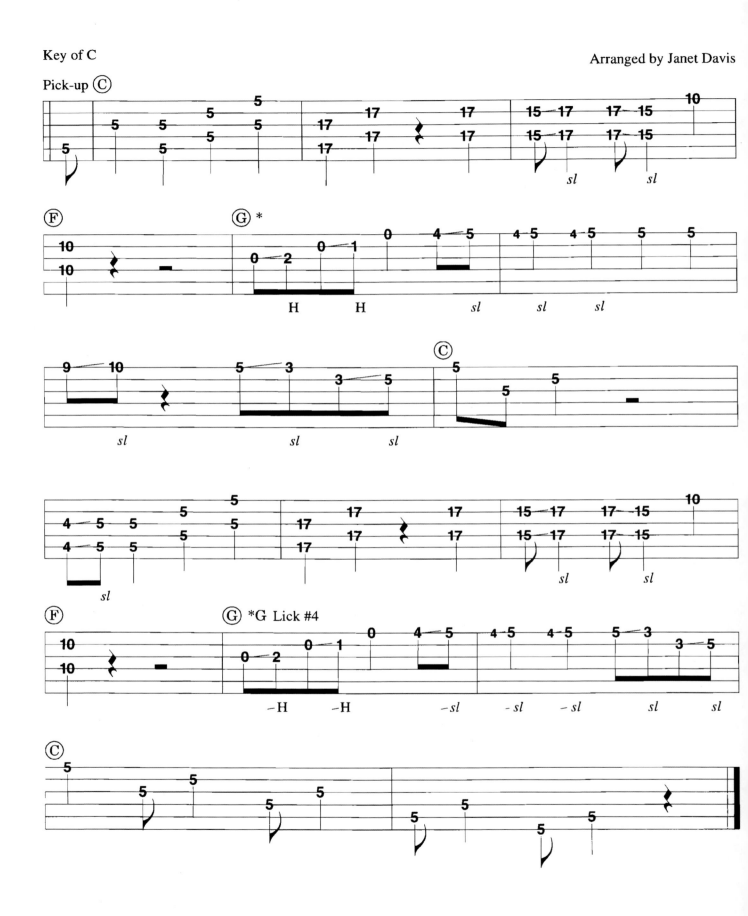

43

• Lesson 13 •
Glissando-The Key of C
"Great Speckled Bird"

Glissando, involves quickly sliding the steel from a low chord position to a high chord position on the fingerboard, sounding all of the tones in between. The glissando can also be executed in reverse, going from a high chord to a low chord (in pitch or fret number). Technically, this produces rapid scales on each string, which lead the ear of the listener to the higher chord. *Great Speckled Bird* uses the glissando technique to connect the F chords at the 10th fret and at the 22nd fret. (Emphasize the first chord and the last chord.)

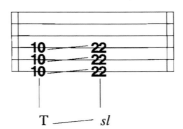

KEY OF C:

This tune is played in the Key of C. Therefore, the primary chords will be the **C, F, and G chords.** It helps to locate the primary chord positions before you begin to actually play through the arrangement. (Hint: The F chord is two frets lower than the G Chord.)

44

Great Speckled Bird

45

• Lesson 14 •
Slant Chord
"Dark Hollow" using closed positions

In *Dark Hollow,* measure 2 introduces a slant chord. (See pg. 13 for picture.) Notice that the steel covers two different fret numbers in a slant chord.

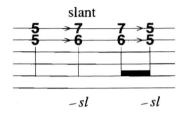

To play the Forward Slant Chord:

1.) Move your left index finger to the side of the steel;
2.) Angle the bar so that it covers the two frets indicated over the first two strings. (Because these are the only strings you will pick, don't be concerned with the other frets the bar has to cover.)

NOTE: Angle or turn the bar with your fingers — NOT your wrist. The left wrist should not change its angle. Obviously, your fingers will have to readjust themselves to control the bar. Your left index should move to the side of the steel from the top. Be sure the bar is precisely over the metal fret bars of each fret indicated for the chord.

NOTE: The bar usually slides into and out of slanted chords; don't lift the bar off of the strings between the barre chord and the slant chord.

CLOSED CHORD LICK #2:

The closed chord lick #2, introduced in *Home In Dixie* also occurs in this arrangement for *Dark Hollow.* Again, remember that a closed chord lick is a pattern that can be used for any chord. The lick #2 is usually used to end the song. (The last chord in the Key of C will usually be the C chord.)

UP THE NECK:

Notice that this arrangment moves up the neck for the C chord (17th fret). These same notes could also be played from the 5th fret C chord position.

KEY OF C:

Dark Hollow is played in the Key of C. Therefore, the primary chords are the C, F, and G chords. Refer back to *Home In Dixie, Footprints In the Snow,* and *Great Speckled Bird,* and notice the chords for those tunes; they also use this set of chords, (C,F, &G). Each of these songs is played in the Key of C.

NOTES: _____

1.) In *Dark Hollow,* the slant chord is used to harmonize the melody note. Slant chords can also be used as a neighbor chords to add interest and/or color. Another use is as passing chords when traveling from one chord to another. We will cover these uses in the slower songs presented later on.

Dark Hollow

Key of C
Standard Tuning

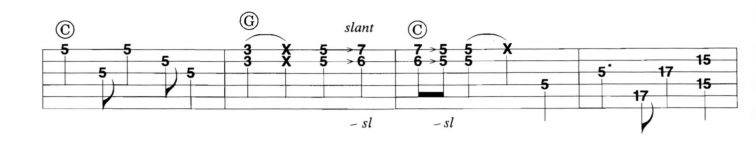

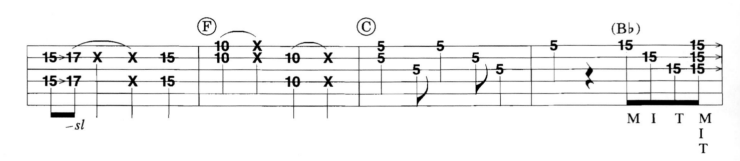

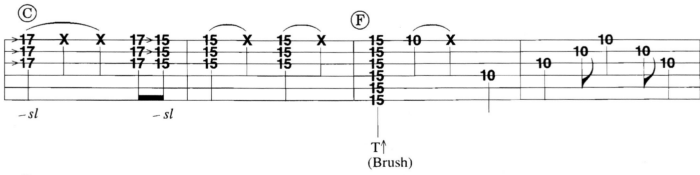

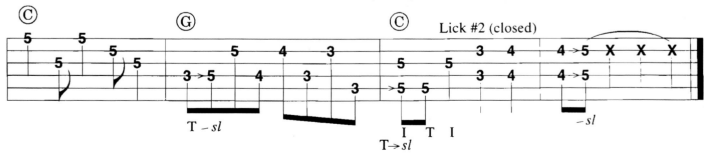

47

• Lesson 15 •
Playing by Ear
HELPFUL HINTS FOR FINDING THE CHORDS TO A SONG*

When you first try to pick out a song, where do you start?

1.) Find a chord position and try to pick the melody notes out around this position. Whatever chord you begin with will be the main chord for the song (usually). **i.e.** G chord is the home chord for the Key of G; the C chord usually begins songs in the Key of C.

2.) When this stops working, how do you find the next chord? To figure out the other two primary chords, (there are only three primary chords), count up the alphabet on your fingers from the chord you started with, to the 4th & 5th chord name letters. For example: count the chord from step 1 as #1.

i.e. Start with the (G) chord as #1:   1 2 3 4 5   1 2 3 4 5
Primary Chords in **Key of G** (bolded)   **G** A B **C D**   **C** D E **F G** = Key of C

3.) If the three primary chords don't work*, try each of the other chords in the scale: i.e. A, B & E for Key of G, or D E A for Key of C. Although these may be played as minor chords, the melody notes can be found around the basic major chord positions.

4.) Every song can be played in any key. Songs almost always end on the chord named for the key (C chord for Key of C). If you are playing along with a recording, the last chord will give you a home chord from which to figure out the other chords.

For Practice: Thumb through the songs in this book, and notice what chords are used for each song. The *key* for the song is noted in the upper left corner of the page. Check to see if the *last* chord in the song matches the name of the key. Does the song begin with this chord? Check to see if the *first* chord matches the key name. You may find exceptions to the beginning chord, but it should be a primary chord nevertheless. See if you can find which song does *not* begin with the chord named for the key of the song. Hint: this song occurs several times in this book. (See "Notes" below for answer.)

Also, practice figuring out the primary chords for the various keys using the method described above, (by counting to five on your fingers for the 1st, 4th, & 5th chords): 1.) Choose a song and look at the key name; try to name the chords before looking at the chord indications over the tablature. 2.) Next, look only at the chord symbols in a song, and try to name the key to which that set of chords belongs...this is the key in which the song is being played.

The above techniques will help you when you are working out songs on your own. In addition, they will come in handy when you get together with other musicians. You will find it easier to play with them. If they tell you the key a song is in, you should be able to figure out the primary chords & play along.

NOTES: _____

1.) It is not necessary to understand the "helpful hints" in order to play the songs in this book. However, when you start trying to pick out songs on your own, these will really help. If they don't make sense right now, keep on going, and return to these hints at a later time. You should derive new information from this book each time you go through it, as your musical knowledge and understanding increase.

2.) Remember, the musical alphabet uses A through G only — (no H).

3.) *John Hardy* starts on the 4th chord of the key.

• Lesson 16 •
Finding the Melody On One String
"Wabash Cannonball"

You can also pick out the melody notes for a song along just one string of the resophonic guitar by tilting the bar and fretting only those notes. Virtually any song can be played this way. (Many bluegrass songs are played in this manner.)

To pick out the melody for *Wabash Cannonball,* use just the first string, and try to play the tune. You can use your ear to help you locate the notes, or you can use the notes from the G scale line (see bottom of page) as a guide from which to choose the melody notes. (The tune for any song played in the Key of G will draw from this set of notes.) A basic arrangement is demonstrated *on the following page.*

If you don't understand the theory presented below at this time, just use your ear to pick out the melody, for the time being. This is to be expected, but if you will read through it, you will find that it will make sense later on.

NOTES: _____

1.) There is a simple mathematical way to find melody notes:

You can simply use your ear to guide you to find the notes, or you can use the scale line to locate the main notes in a song. The melody or tune for a song uses the set of notes which belongs to the scale which is named for the key for the song. (*Scala* means *ladder* in Latin.)

The following diagram includes all of the notes which belong to the G Major Scale, which is used for the Key of G. The melody for a song played in the Key of G will use this set of notes.

(Which notes are up to the composer.) The chords for the song will also use this set of notes.

When you start this scale from the letter G, you will find that the scale uses a fingerboard pattern called an "interval" pattern (distance from one note to the next). Notice that some notes are 2 frets apart, while others are 1 fret apart. The interval pattern (fret distance between each note) for any major scale from its *root* (G) is like a phone number: 2 - 2 - 1 - 2 - 2 - 2 - 1. (See 3rd string, below.)

THE G MAJOR SCALE TONES on the Fretboard:
— Notes used to play songs in the Key of G —

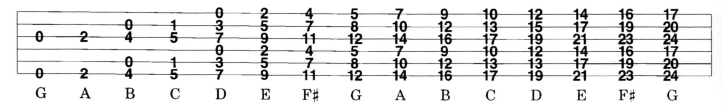

| G | A | B | C | D | E | F♯ | G | A | B | C | D | E | F♯ | G |

Notice on the resophonic guitar, that the same notes are played on the:
3rd & 6th strings,   2nd & 5th strings,   1st and 4th strings.
On the deep string, the note is the same pitch, but an octave lower.

NOTES: _____

1.) If a note in your song is deeper in pitch than the open string, move to the adjacent string (i.e. from 1st to 2nd string) to find the tone you are looking for.

Wabash Cannonball

Key of G

Pick-up notes:

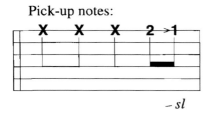

– sl

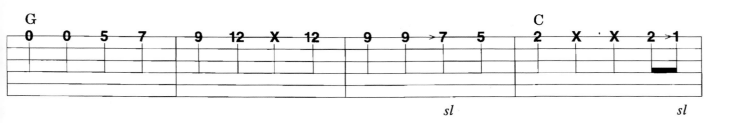

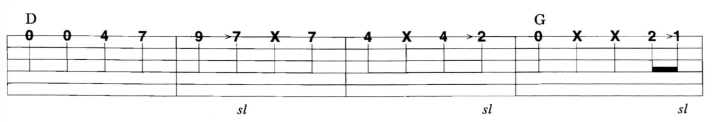

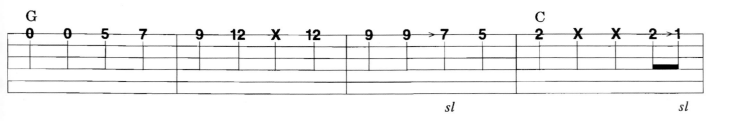

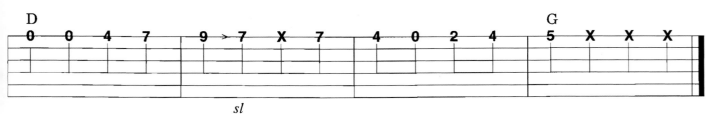

Each 4 measures is like a sentence or a line of poetry. In music, each "sentence" is called a phrase. Notice that the 1st and 3rd phrases are alike in *Wabash Cannonball*. This is common in many songs. Therefore, you can play the same notes, licks, etc. for the 1st & 3rd lines.

• Lesson 17 •
Embellishing The Melody
"Wabash Cannonball"

Hopefully, you now realize that the main melody notes for a song can be found along a single string and also within or close to the chord positions indicated. (For examples of each, see *Wabash Cannonball*, pg. 50 & pg. 32.) Resophonic guitar players often use a combination of these techniques to incorporate the tune. For example, in *Wabash Cannonball*, you may find it easier to play the notes for the D chord (mm. 5-7) from the barred D chord position.

i.e. **D**

D

SLIDES: Resophonic guitar players frequently *slide* into or out of the melody notes to add embellishment. Generally, you should slide only 1 or 2 frets. Too much sliding causes the arrangement to lose stability, and may make the listener dizzy. When using this technique, you can slide to a melody note from a higher pitched neighbor tone or from a lower pitched tone. The slide leads the music into the melody note and teases the ear of the listener into wanting to hear the desired tone. It also utilizes the timbre or tone quality characteristic of the DOBRO®. Notice the slides used for the melody notes in the C chord in the following arrangement for *Wabash Cannonball* (m. 4). Hold the steel precisely over the metal fret, so that your pitch is accurate.

LICKS are very effective for embellishing an arrangement. They are particularly useful at the end of a break, to add excitement and drive to the close of the arrangement. Each of the following is a single-string lick* which can be played for the G chord at the close of *Wabash Cannonball*. Once you learn these licks, you can use them in many different songs.

G Lick #1* (*Salty Dog* pg. 29)

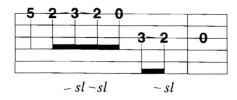

G Lick #2 (*Wabash Cannonball* pg. 32)

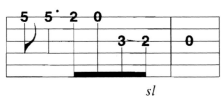

Combination of G licks: (Combined, these make a good ending.)
Lick #5   Lick #6   Lick #7

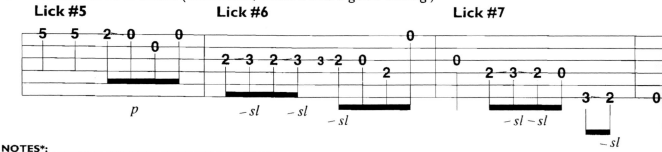

NOTES*: _____

1.) These are *not closed chord licks*; they are *only* used for a certain chord due to their inclusion of the open strings.

2.) The above licks can *also* be used as G chord fill-in licks *within* a song.

Wabash Cannonball

• Lesson 18 •
Vibrato
"John Henry"

Vibrato is a technique used to help *sustain* a tone for a longer duration. This is much like the technique vocalists use with their vocal cords. Vibrato is caused on the resophonic guitar by rapidly moving the steel bar back and forth over the metal fret bar. The oscillation from the steel causes the note to continue ringing (vibrating) beyond its normal decay time.

The notes which are usually sustained by vibrato are those which should continue ringing for more than one beat, (the notes which are followed by x's in the tablature).

To achieve the vibrato, some people move the bar as far as $\frac{1}{2}$ fret in either direction. However, take care not to get too far out of the accurate pitch for the note you are playing. ($\frac{1}{8}$" is recommended.)

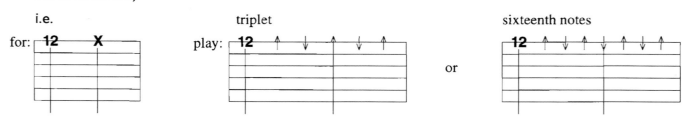

It is important to keep the steel moving at a steady pace. The *rate* of the bar oscillation for the vibrato is up to you...*experiment, until it sounds right* to you. The above examples use 3 slides per beat and 4 per beat. You can also double the number of oscillations. You can even play as if you have a tremor in your right hand, but try to keep the bar moving steadily.

In *John Henry*, try using the vibrato technique for each note followed by an X in the first two measures. This song is played in the Key of D, using the D & A chords. This arrangement also demonstrates the techniques for playing the melody along a single string as well as from the chord positions, (discussed with *Wabash Cannonball*).

Before playing through the song, look for patterns. For example, find measures that match. This will make it easier to learn the song. Also isolate patterns to practice by themselves, which you can use in other songs.

1.) Notice that the first line and the third line are basically alike.
2.) Notice that several of the measures are based around the 7th fret (D chord).
3.) The 3rd measure is a D lick (closed chord pattern).
   Remember to use vibrato to sustain the notes followed by the X's.

IMPORTANT NOTES: _____

1.) Vibrato is commonly associated with Hawaiian-style DOBRO®, and with most slow tunes. However, it is also effective when you want to sustain a single note in a tune played at a fast tempo, as in *John Henry*.
2.) Vibrato can also be used when picking 2 or more notes simultaneously.
3.) The oscillation should be continuous regardless of the rate; do not stop between the beats.
4.) Too much vibrato throughout a song may cause the DOBRO® to sound out of tune. Experiment; try to relate this technique to a vocalist. The "right" amount can be very beautiful, whereas too much can ruin the overall effect you are trying to achieve.
5.) Vibrato can also be a useful tool to cover a note that is initially played out of tune.

53

John Henry

Key of D
Standard Tuning

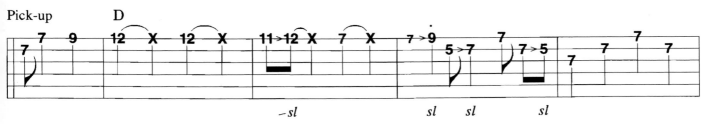

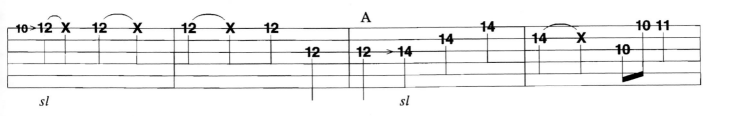

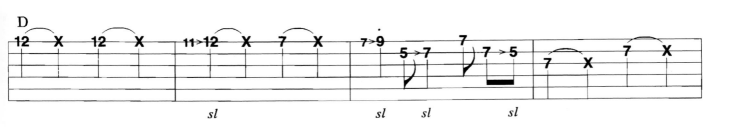

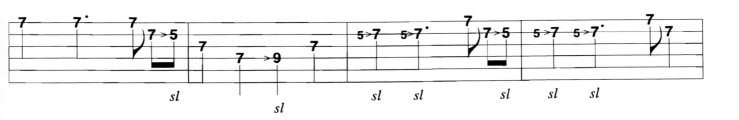

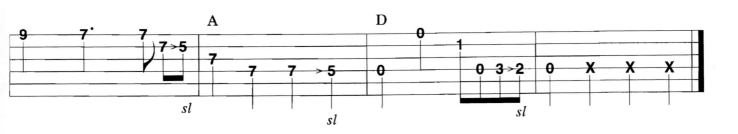

$\dot{9}$ = a dot above a note means to stop the tone w/left finger, after picking it with the right hand; this should have a sharp, *staccato* effect. Do not sustain this note.

• Lesson 19 •
Open-String Licks – Tilting the Bar

Many bluegrass arrangements for the resophonic guitar involve *tilting* the steel, so that only the tip of the bar will fret one string at a time. In these songs, the melody notes are often incorporated into *open-string* licks throughout the song. Usually this type of lick involves playing a combination of open strings and fretted notes on a single strings. It is important to remember that each open-string lick is played only for a *certain* chord. (You have already learned examples of this type of lick; i.e. the final G chord in *Salty Dog, Wabash Cannonball,* and *Cripple Creek* {G licks 1, 2 & 3}.)

Notice in the arrangement on the following page, that many of the open G chord licks *will slide from the 2 - 4 frets* and also from the *4 - 2 frets* on the *3rd string* and that the open D chord lick will slide from the 2 - 4 and back on the *4th string*. As we have discussed previously, resophonic guitar players often slide into the melody notes from 2 frets away for the sake of embellishment.

G

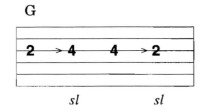

D

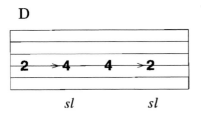

It is important to realize that a song is a series of chords. Many songs will use the same chords. A song that is played in the Key of G will usually use the G, C, and D chords as the primary chords. The chords for a song plus the sequence in which the chords are played are referred to as a *chord progression.* The arrangement on the following page is a chord progression which is common to many different tunes. You can play this as a "break" for *Blue Ridge Cabin Home, Ride 'Em Down Easy, You're Gonna Miss Me When I'm Gone,* and many other songs. The melodies are similar and the chord progressions are identical; therefore, the same licks can be played for each of these songs.

Hint: To play the G lick in the 1st measure (after the pick-up notes):

1.) Tilt the bar so that you fret only the 3rd string at the 2nd fret;
2.) Slide the bar to the 4th fret (remember to drag your left ring and pinky fingers behind the bar);
3.) Lift the bar, followed by your (left) ring and pinky fingers to dampen the sound, in one smooth motion;
4.) With a circular motion, return to the 2nd fret and repeat the slide;
5.) Practice this left-hand technique over and over until you can repeat this slide smoothly and evenly, for it will be used in many songs.

NOTES: _____

1.) You do not have to include every melody note in a song in your arrangement. Often, resophonic guitar players play only the most important melody notes.

Chord Progression #1
G, C, D

Key of G

Tab setting by Janet Davis

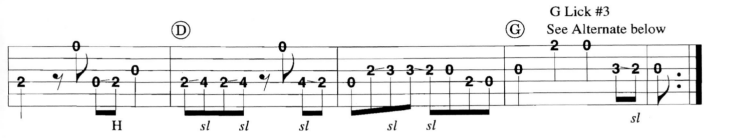

NOTE: ʾ is an eighth rest.
Pause (do not play) for the duration of one eighth note.

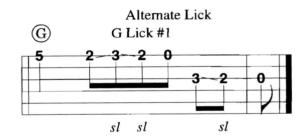

• Lesson 20 •
Chord Progressions

If you are ever called upon to play *Bugle Call Rag*, *Dueling Banjos*, or *Black Mountain Rag*, you will find that you can play the *same* "break" for the fast part of each of these tunes. These songs use an identical chord progression. In bluegrass music, the same licks can often be used to play different songs that don't really have a singable tune, as long as they have the same chord progression. (Many songs of this type, {i.e. breakdowns} are identifiable primarily by their introductory section, {such as the harmonics at the beginning of *Bugle Call Rag*}.)

A chord progression includes a set of specific chords to be played in a specific order, with *each* chord lasting through a specific number of measures. In this case, you play something for the C chord for two measures*, then two measures of G chord notes, followed by two measures of D licks, and finally two measures for the G chord. In other words, the following chord progressions consists of:

C = 2mm + G = 2mm + D = 2mm + G = 2mm

As you learn "licks" which work for the G chord, you can use them in any song, when the G chord occurs. Likewise, when learning a new song, notice what you play for the D chord, and substitute this (lick) in other songs when the D chord occurs.

i.e. Notice the *G lick* which is played for measures 7 & 8, and again for mm. 15 & 16. *Substitute* this for the final G chord in Chord Progression #1. Now go to *Salty Dog*, and substitute this lick for the last G chord lick...(yes, it begins with the 3rd string). When learning *Sunnyvale Breakdown*, try substituting this lick for its final G chord.

G LICK #7:

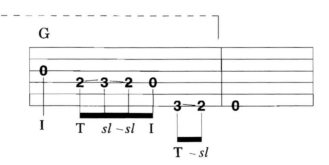

Are you beginning to understand how important chords are? Even when the bar doesn't appear to be forming a chord position, you will be playing notes that work for a certain chord.* Many of these note combinations are patterns which can be played for the same chord in other songs. Recurring patterns are an important key to improvisation.

As you become aware of chord progressions, you will begin to notice that the same ones are often used for different songs.

NOTES: _____

1.) *Musicians often refer to this as "playing over a chord."

2.) The actual "lick" consists of only the measure. The note *after* the barline resolves the lick, but is not part of it. (It begins another lick.)

57

Chord Progression #2
C, G, D, G

Key of G

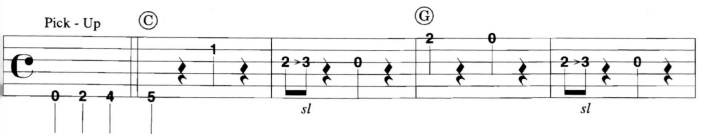

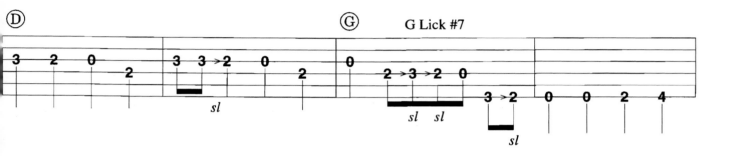

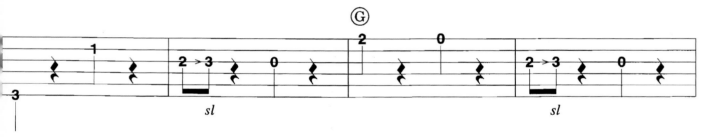

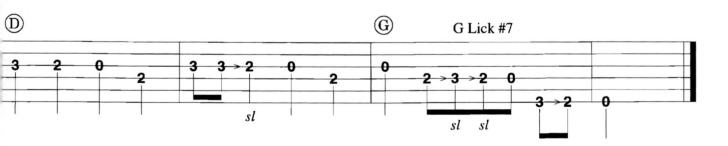

EXAMPLE: Introduction (Usually played by Banjo)

Harmonics

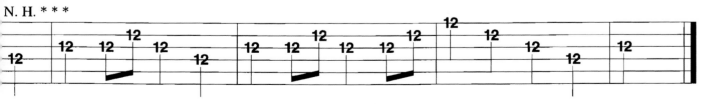

• Lesson 21 •
The "Foggy Mountain" Lick

This lick is used to begin many bluegrass breakdowns. It can be used for both the G chord and for the D chord*. Notice that the slide technique is used twice in a row. This is a variation of the forward roll pattern.

G LICK #8

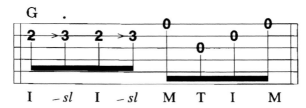

1.) *Lift the bar* after the first slide;

2.) Return to the 2nd fret & slide to the 3rd fret again.

3.) Remember to *dampen the string* with your left ring finger as you lift the bar to avoid any rattle from the string.

In the song *Train 45,* notice that:

1.) **G Lick #8,** above, is played three times in a row.
(The 3rd measure varies one note, leading the lick into its resolution.)

2.) **G Lick #3** (*Cripple Creek* lick) occurs in measure 5:
This is another commonly used lick for the G chord.

3.) **G Lick #9:** In the variation for *Train 45:* Cover the 1st *and* 2nd strings with the bar over the 2nd fret; then slide to the 3rd fret as you did above.

NOTES: _____

1.) The G chord and the D chord both include the "d" tone (open 1st and 4th strings). Licks which emphasize this tone will often work for either chord.

Train 45

Key of G

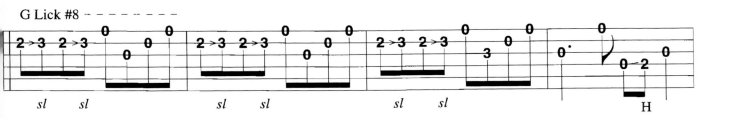

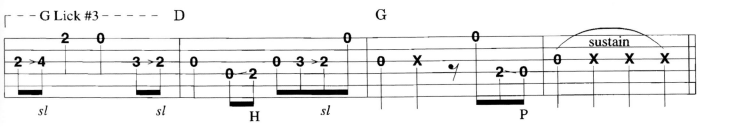

Variation

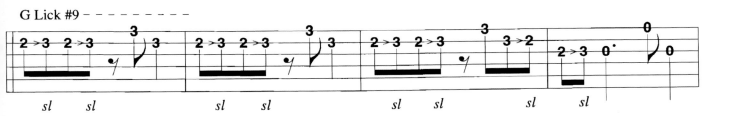

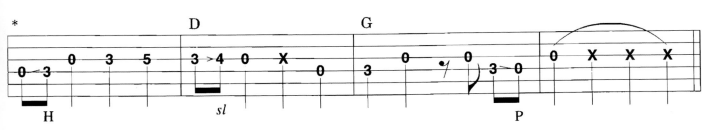

* or play 2nd line of top arrangement.

• Lesson 22 •
Combining Licks
"Sunnyvale Breakdown"

Notice that the tune on the following page begins with the *Foggy Mountain* lick (G Lick #8), which was used to begin *Train 45*. Before playing the song, look over the tablature, measure by measure, and pick out the licks you have learned. Look for the *Cripple Creek lick* (G#3) in this arrangement. How many times does it occur? (The final G lick is also a variation of this lick.)

D Lick #1:

This is a new lick which can be played for the *D* chord in many different songs. Notice that it consists of two measures, so it actually combines two D licks.

Lift the steel after the first 2-3 slide, releasing your ring/pinky fingers last to stop the tone, then repeat the slide. This is the same technique used for the *Foggy Mountain* lick.

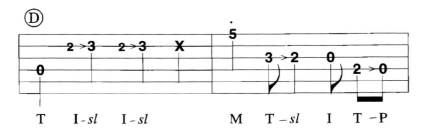

A summary ... so far

As you gain experience by playing several different songs on the resophonic guitar, you will begin to find similarities among all of the songs. So far, we have discovered the fact that different songs can use the same roll patterns and licks, and they may also use the same chords.

NOTES: _____

1.) The *Cripple Creek* lick occurs 3 times in *Sunnyvale Breakdown*, (m. 3, m. 7, & m. 11).
2.) Although *Sunnyvale Breakdown* begins with the same lick used for *Train 45*, the two songs sound completely different, primarily to the difference in chord progressions.
3.) Tilt the bar for the C chord notes.
4.) If you want to play *Foggy Mountain Breakdown*, simply substitute the E minor chord where the C chord measures occur.

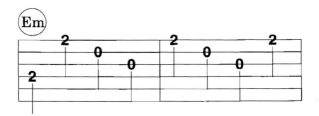

Sunnyvale Breakdown

• Lesson 23 •
Interchanging Licks
"Train 45"

By now, you should be fairly adept at playing G lick #3, which was introduced in *Cripple Creek* and appeared again in *Train 45* and *Sunnyvale Breakdown*.

G LICK #3 (also called the *Cripple Creek Lick*):

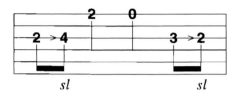

The following lick embellishes upon the above lick and is useful when you want to add more drive to a passage in a song. Notice that the opening slide is a fast slide.

The 2-3 slide should occur in the same amount of time one eighth note is played. ♪ = ♫

G LICK #10:

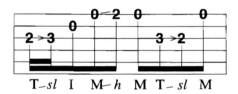

T–*sl* I M–*h* M T–*sl* M

NOTE: This lick was used in Part B of *Blackberry Blossom* for the G chord. For practice, locate the lick and play through it, isolating it from the rest of the song.

These two licks are interchangeable in any song.

In the following variation for *Train 45:*

  1.) Locate each occurrence of the above licks.
  2.) After you learn to play the arrangement, try interchanging these licks. i.e. play lick 3 for lick 10, and vice versa.
  3.) *Experiment* to see which way you like to play it.

Now play Cripple Creek, substituting Lick #10 where you normally play Lick #3.

Are you beginning to see how to improvise?

NOTES: _____

  1.) In measure 6 of each variation of *Train 45* on the following page, you will also find interchangeable D licks which can be played for the D chord in any song. For fun, substitute each D lick below for m. 6 in the previous version of *Train 45*, which you already played. You can "keep" any of these for your own arrangement.

D Lick #2   **D Lick #3**   **D Lick #4**

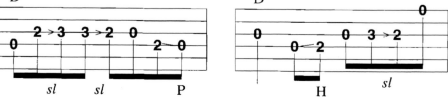

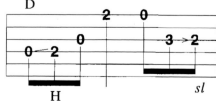

Train 45

Key of G

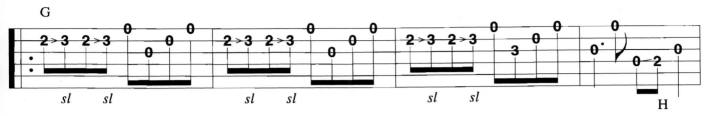

*G Lick #10   D Lick #3

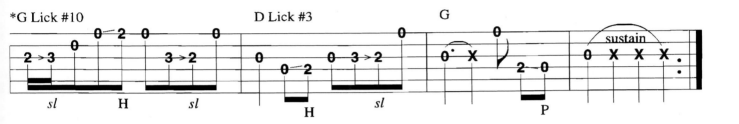

Variation

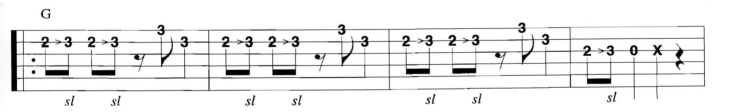

*G Lick #10   D Lick #2

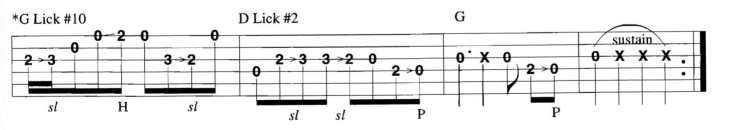

Note: The first line of each arrangement is the same as on pg. 60. Only the 2nd line has changed.

• Lesson 24 •
Natural Harmonics (chimes):
"Grandfather's Clock"

Natural harmonics are bell-like overtones which are produced on the resophonic guitar without using the steel bar. These harmonics are produced by lightly touching the open string, dividing it exactly in ½, or ⅓, or ¼, etc. with the left hand while picking the string with the right hand. In Grandfather's Clock, natural harmonics are used to imitate the clock chiming in Part C.

To produce pure, clear harmonics:

1.) *Lightly* touch the outside edge of the palm of your left hand across the 12th fret*, right over the metal bar. Do not depress the string. Do not use the steel bar!

2.) *Pick* the 1st string with your right hand

3.) *Immediately lift* your left hand off of the string, in order to allow the chime to ring. This is extremely important!

You can easily play natural harmonics over the 12th, 7th, & 5th frets. (See page 18 for pictures and a more thorough explanation.)

Natural harmonics can be produced in this manner on any string or combination of strings at the 12th fret, (dividing the string in ½). By playing harmonics on several strings at the 12th fret, you will be playing a G chord using overtones. You can also play the same overtones for the G chord an octave higher at the 5th fret, (dividing the string into ¼). The D chord can be produced at the 7th fret (dividing the string by ⅓).

GRANDFATHER'S CLOCK: For fun, after you learn to play Grandfather's Clock, substitute the 5th fret for the 12th fret when the harmonics occur in Part C. Locate the D chord lick in measure 6. For practice, substitute D Lick #4, below, for this lick. This lick adds a surge of energy to the song as it returns to the G chord.

D Lick #4:

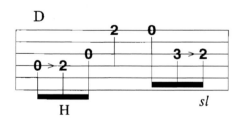

NOTES: _____

1.) Only certain frets will produce this type of harmonics; dividing the string in exact fractional parts is what causes these tones. Harmonics are commonly produced at the 12th fret, 7th fret, and 5th fret. (These divide the string in ½, ⅓, & ¼ respectively.) You can also produce harmonics at the 24th, 19th frets. (Notice that if you play all of the strings, at one fret, you produce the G chord at the 5th and 12th & 24th frets, and a D chord at the 7th & 19th frets.) Harmonics can be played at the 4th, 9th and 16th frets to produce the B chord, but they are more difficult to produce clearly. The 17th also produces a G chord, and the 22nd fret produces an F chord.

Grandfather's Clock

Pick-Up Notes:

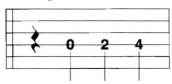

Part A:

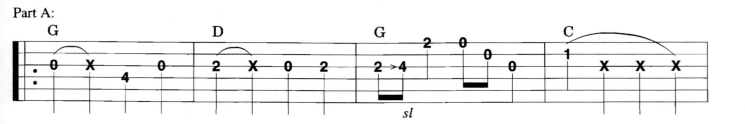

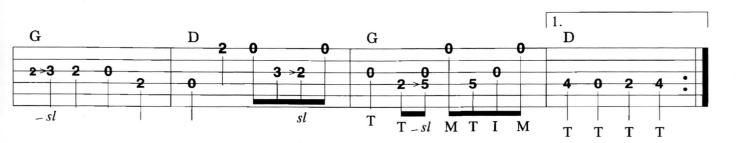

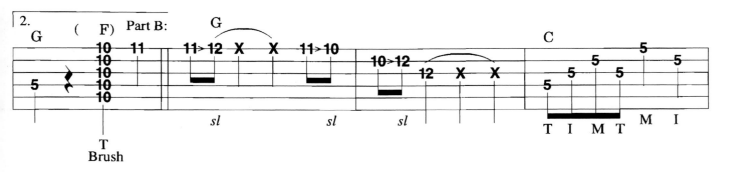

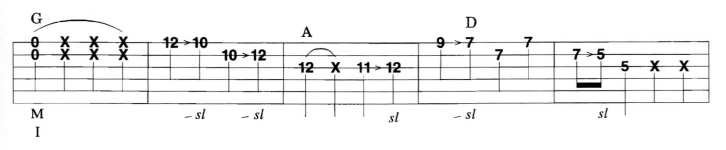

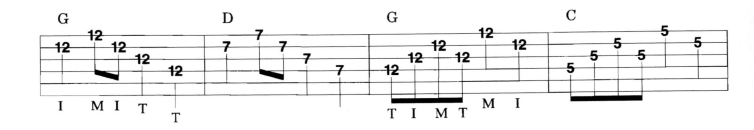

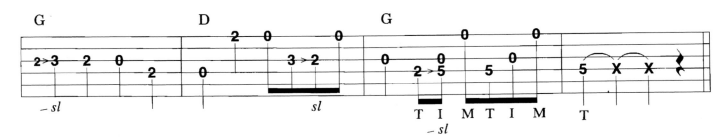

Part C:

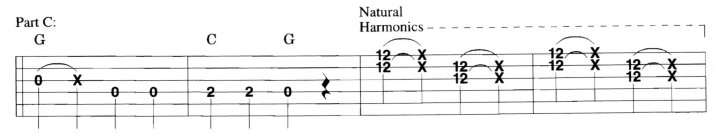

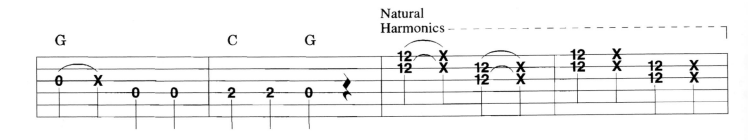

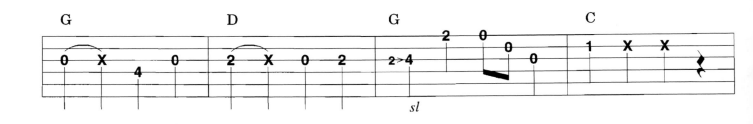

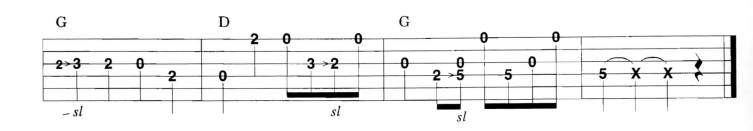

• Lesson 25 •
Interchanging "D" Licks
"Hamilton County Breakdown"

Many of the songs you will play on the resophonic guitar will use the D chord, particularly when they are played in the Key of G. Usually, two measures of the D chord will precede the final G chord. It is useful to have several "D" Licks in your "lick vocabulary," so they are at your fingertips when the D chord occurs in a songs.

The following licks can be substituted for one another in many different songs. *For practice,* substitute D Lick #5 in *Sunnyvale Breakdown.* You can also exchange these licks in *Hamilton County Breakdown* and play D Lick #5 in Part A and D Lick #1 in Part B.

D Lick #1: (used in Part A of *Hamilton County.*)
This is the same D Lick #1 played in *Sunnyvale Breakdown.*

D Lick #5: (used in Part B of *Hamilton County.*)

D Lick #6: (used in alt. Part B of *Hamilton County.*)

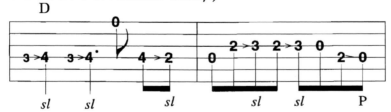

Hamilton County Breakdown is a popular bluegrass tune and fun to play. By now, you should recognize most of the patterns used to play the first arrangement.

Part A: Notice that it begins with the *Foggy Mountain* G Lick.
          Notice that it uses "D" lick #1 from *Sunnyvale Breakdown.*
          The D lick is followed by the now familiar G Lick #3 (*Cripple Creek*).

Part B: Notice that this section uses the chord progression #2 on page 58.
          Therefore, the patterns or licks used for each chord in that arrangement can also be played for the corresponding chord(s) in this tune.

Variation: The variation for Part B provides you with even more licks which can be inter-changed with one another (by chord). The C chord lick can be used in many different songs when the C chord occurs. You can also substitute this for the C chord in the first arrangement for Part B.

NOTES: _____

1.) If a song requires only 1 measure of D chord, play the 2nd measure of the above lick(s). It will lead to the G chord, which usually will follow the D chord. *For practice, substitute the 2nd measure of D Lick #5 for the D chord in "Train 45."*

68

Hamilton County Breakdown

Key of G

Part A:

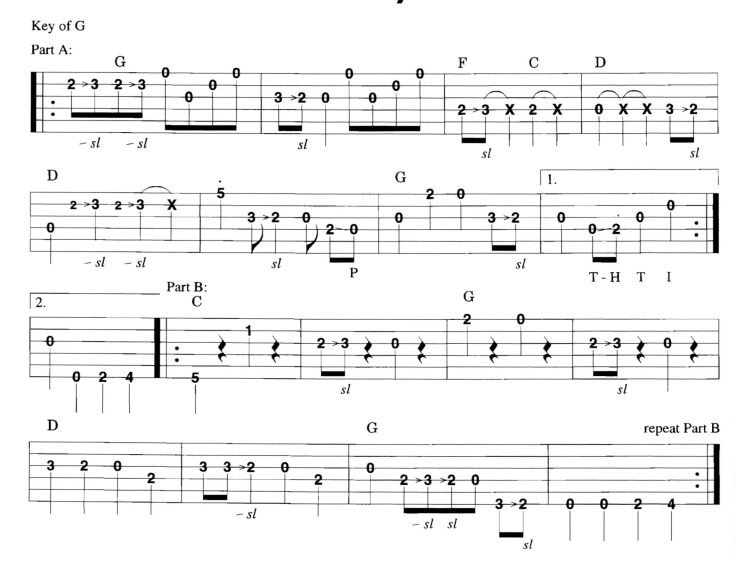

Variation of Part B Only
Substitute for Part B in above arrangement

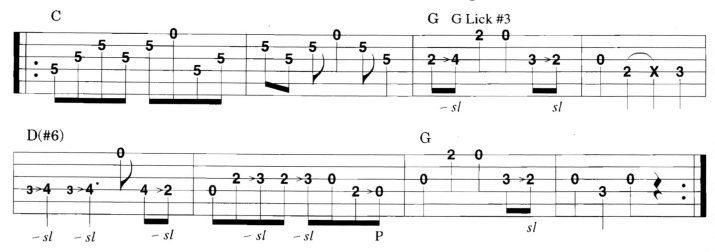

• Lesson 26 •
Seventh Chords
"Hamilton County Breakdown" – Part B

The following is an *alternate* variation for *Part B* of *Hamilton County Breakdown*. By combining this with Part A on the previous page, you will have two different variations for *Hamilton County Breakdown*.

This arrangement uses *seventh chords*. The fingerboard position for a *7th chord* is located *3 frets higher* than the basic barre position of the chord. *Sevenths* can be used to *add color and/or tension* to the basic major chord. (Technically, an extra tone is simply added to the basic chord to form the 7th chord; this tone is the 7th note of the scale named for the chord, flatted.)

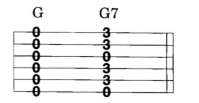

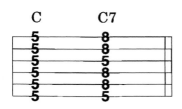

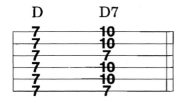

NOTE: usually you will barre only two strings to play the 7th chord.

CLOSED CHORD POSITION LICK #3:

The same closed position lick is played for the C & D chords in this arrangement.

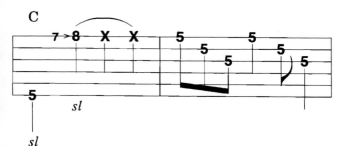

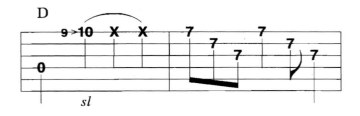

G LICK #11 (open string lick):

This lick can easily be interchanged with G Lick #1 in *Salty Dog*, and with G Lick #2 in *Wabash Cannonball*. Also, try substituting this lick for Lick #5 in the "combination or sequence of licks" on page 51. Notice that it includes the 7th.

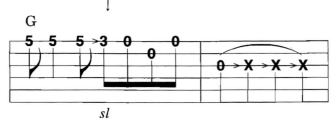

NOTES: _____

1.) Other examples of licks using 7ths can be found in the following:
Variation for *Train 45*, pg. 64, and alt. intro. to *Sunnyvale Breakdown*, pg. 62.

Hamilton County Breakdown
Part B

Key of G
Variation using 7th chords

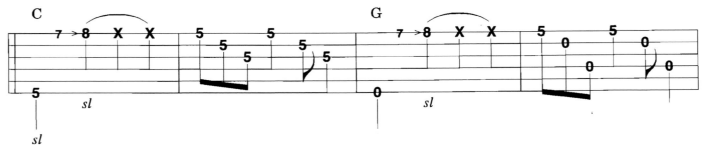

NOTE: Substitute this arrangement for Part B (only) on page 69.

NOTE: ♪ ♩ = short - long.

NOTE: The bluesy effect of this arrangement is due to the addition of the "7th note" to the basic major chords.

• Lesson 27 •
Closed Chord Blues Licks
"John Hardy"

In Lesson 8, *John Hardy* demonstrated how a single lick pattern which is built around a barred chord position can be used for different chords. This, as you know, is achieved by moving the steel to the appropriate chord position and playing the same fingerboard pattern. The following arrangement of *John Hardy* will be based upon that arrangement, but will replace the "closed chord lick #1" with a "closed seventh chord lick pattern." Remember, seventh chords add both color and tension to a song. They can add drive as well as produce a bluesy effect.

The following lick uses the two notes on the 1st and 2nd strings located 3 frets higher (in pitch) than the basic chord.* Closed seventh chord lick patterns are generally played on two adjacent strings, three frets higher (in pitch) than the basic chord position. The following lick is played in measures 9, 10, 13, and 14. Notice how it causes the listener to feel that something is about to happen. (The audience would feel pretty distressed if the song were to end on the D chord, without the resolution to the final G chord.) This is a great lick for adding drive to a song.

CLOSED LICK #4:

C Lick

I– sl   I– sl   M   I

D Lick

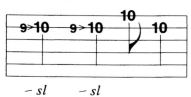

– sl   – sl

G Lick

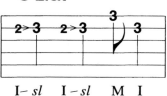

I– sl   I– sl   M   I

NOTES: _____

1.) The D chord for *John Hardy* uses a combination of **three** 2-measure D Licks.
2.) *This lick pattern is played from the "7th chord position" for the basic chord.
3.) The term *closed* means that all of the notes in the lick are fretted; open strings are not used in the lick.
4.) For more information on 7th chords, see pg. 70.
5.) *Learned as G Lick #9.

John Hardy

Key of G

Note: **7→8** = quick slide

• Lesson 28 •
Syncopation and Blues Notes
"Train 45" Up-the-Neck

The following arrangement for *Train 45* is a culmination of many of the techniques which have been covered so far. The first two lines are played up-the-neck in the style of *John Henry*. The ( ) have replaced the X's to indicate a *strong vibrato* for these notes.

Footprints in the Snow demonstrated the fact that the fingerboard repeats itself starting at the 12th fret. The 17th fret and the 5th fret of the 1st string produce the same tone (G). However, the tone from the 17th fret is an octave higher. To find the same note on a string in the up-the-neck area, simply add 12 to the fret number of the note: i.e. 5th fret + 12 fret higher = 17th fret. Notice that the 3rd & 4th lines of the song imitate the up-the-neck section, but they are played 12 frets lower (in pitch or fret number).

This arrangement also makes use of the 7ths of the G & D chords to add a bluesy effect. The flat 7th tone of the scale for the chord is the note on the 1st string (and on the 4th string). Two frets higher and you have the root* of the same chord.
Therefore: open   3 → 5   on the 1st string all work for the G chord.
Likewise: 12 —— 15 → 17 on the 1st string work for the G chord, too.
Notice that *Train 45* plays with these notes when it calls for the G chord.

D Lick #4 is used at the end of the song, driving the music back to the G chord. This is a good lick to use when you have only 1 measure of the D chord.

D Lick #4:

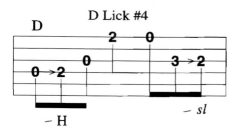

The *"pattern"* indicated above the 1st measure of line 2 is used to produce played a syncopated rhythmic sequence of 3 identical patterns. Notice that the pattern is played 3 times in a row. They are syncopated because the middle pattern in the sequence crosses through the bar line. In other words, three patterns fit into two measures. This is a fun technique to play with when improvising.

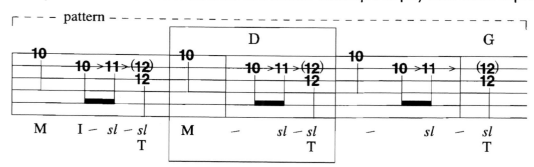

NOTES:_____

1.) The note located 2 frets higher than the 7th of the chord on the 1st string and on the 4th string, is also a tone belonging to the chord. This tone is the root of the chord (G tone for G chord).

2.) In the pattern on line 2, notice that it is played over the G chord and the D chord. These two chords have certain tones in common which make this effective.

Train 45

Key of G
(Capo 4th fret to
play in key of B)

( ) = optional note

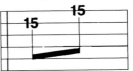

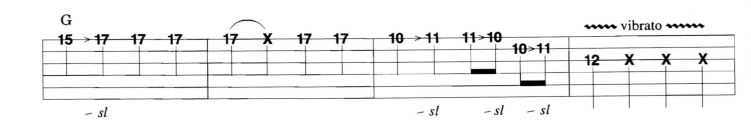

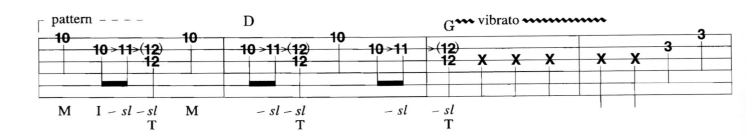

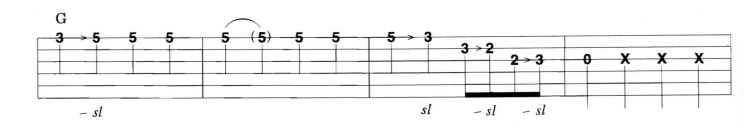

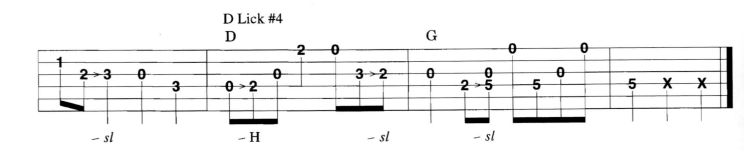

75

• Lesson 29 •
Adding Blues Notes and Harmonics
"Reuben"

Reuben is an extremely popular tune among bluegrass musicians. Notice that almost every measure is played for the D chord. It is a lot of fun to improvise over a single chord. For example, you can play notes that work for the chord in different areas of the fingerboard. On the following page are three variations for *Reuben*.

The **first variation** establishes the tune for the song, and is fairly straightforward.

The **second variation** expands upon this by adding blues notes and color tones. A "blues effect" is caused by altering the position of an expected note, usually by flatting the note. To flat a note, simply bar the note 1 fret lower (in pitch). We have already discussed playing the flat 7th of the scale to form 7th chords. You can also flat 3rds & 6ths (of the major scale), for a bluesy effect.

The *D7 chord* is used for the first measure of the 2nd variation.

The notes belonging to the D7 chord include the basic D major chord at the 7th fret *plus* the two notes on the 1st & 2nd strings at the 10th fret. It also moves up the neck, adding more tension with the higher pitched notes.

D LICK: **D7th chord tones:**

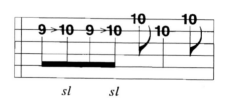
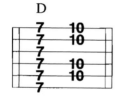

Notice that this D lick is a variation of the "Foggy Mountain" Lick.

The **third variation** is played with *natural harmonics,* (except for the closing licks). Play the chimes by placing the side of your left palm, (or little finger) across the 7th fret...do not place the steel bar on the strings for these notes. At the 7th fret, the natural harmonics play a D chord. (You can also produce D chord chimes across the 19th fret.)

This tune is played in the **Key of D**. Therefore the home chord is the D chord. When a song is played in the Key of D, the primary chords are D, G, and A; these are the 1st, 4th, and 5th notes from the D major scale, upon which the chords are formed.

NOTES: _____

1.) The D7 chord is simply an extension of the basic D major chord; it adds the flatted 7th tone of the D scale to the basic D chord.

2.) To play a 7th chord, play the basic major chord plus the two notes located 3 frets higher on the 1st and 2nd strings. i.e. D7 chord = barre 7th fret + 10th fret; C7 = barre 5th fret + 8th fret notes; G7 = open + 3rd fret.

Reuben

Variation 1

Key of D

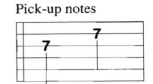

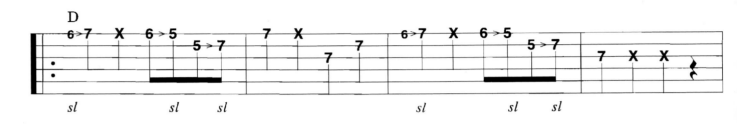

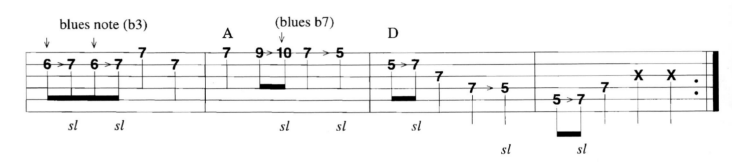

Variation 2

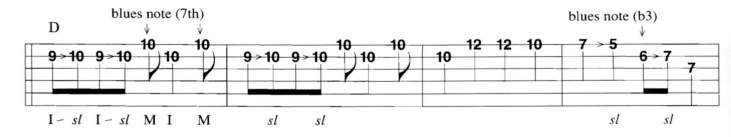

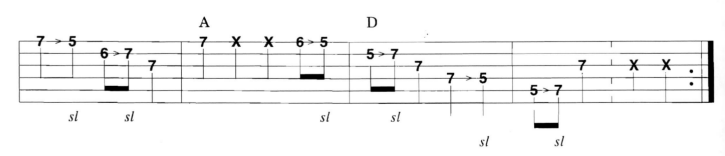

Variation 3

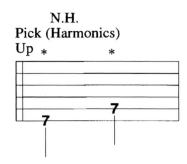

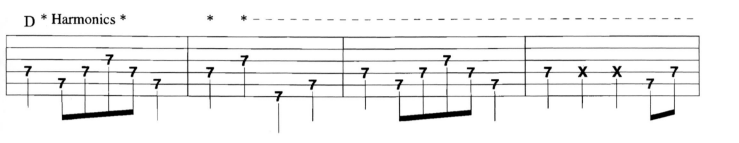

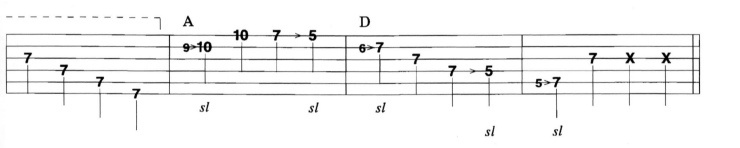

• Lesson 30 •
Using a Capo
"Salt River"

Fiddle players, mandolin players, and bass players often learn to play a song in a *specific key*. The tuning for these instruments makes it smoother and easier to play in certain keys. Also, a vocalist customarily sings in a key that suits his vocal range. Normally, *Salt River*, a well-known bluegrass and fiddle tune, is played in the Key of A. Also, *Cripple Creek is usually played* in the Key of A. Resophonic guitar players often will learn these songs in the Key of G (out of the open position). Then they add the capo on the 2nd fret, so that the song will sound the pitches belonging to the Key of A.

When you use a capo, the capo becomes the nut of the resophonic guitar. Therefore, you should play the song exactly as you did without the capo, but your left-hand position will be moved up two frets, due to the capo. The tones of the resophonic guitar are higher in pitch, putting the song in the Key of A. (Without the capo, the song is in the Key of G.)

Salt River is divided into two sections, just like *Cripple Creek:* Part A should be played twice, and Part B should also be played twice. This is a common form for many traditional fiddle tunes, as is playing in the Key of A. Notice also that this tune calls for the *F chord.*

Single notes in F chord: **Barre Chord:**

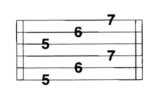

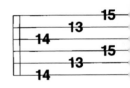

Hint: Learn *Salt River* just as it is written, without the capo. Then place the capo over the 2nd fret, to shorten the neck; you should play from this point as *if it were the nut.* The capo will automatically transpose the song on the resophonic guitar to the Key of A.

Notes: _____

1.) In order to be able to use the open strings, many songs are played in the Key of G, which works well with the open G tuning. If the song is not written for the Key of G, the capo will change the pitch as follows:

   For the Key of G: no capo
   Key of A: capo on 2nd fret
   Key of B♭: capo on 3rd fret
   Key of B : capo on 4th fret
   Key of C: capo on 5th fret
   Key of D: capo on 7th fret

   Notice that the keys correspond to your barre chord position.

2.) The Key of A will be the most common for using the capo.

3.) There are many different types of capos on the market. The elastic capo is inexpensive, but it wears out. The Kyser, Shubb, and the Leno are also excellent capos. These should be available from bluegrass mail-order companies or from your local music store.

4.) You do not have to have a capo to play the following arrangement. However, it is time to begin using your capo if you have one.

Salt River

Standard G Tuning
Capo 2nd fret for Key of A

Part A:

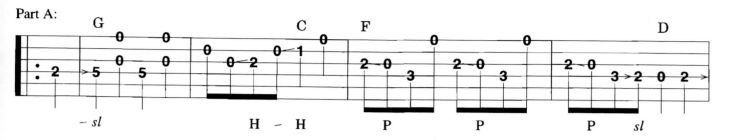

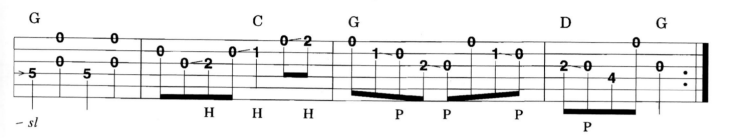

Part B:

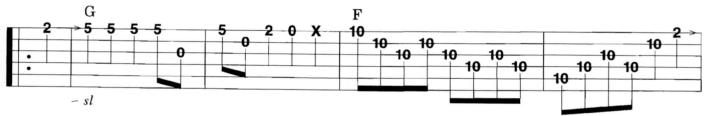

*see alternate lick

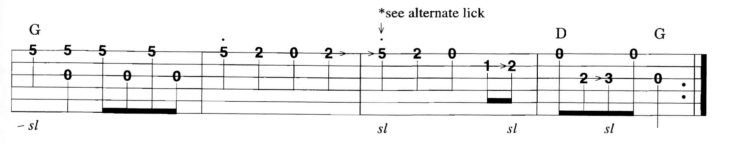

Alternate ending lick: (tilt bar)
G*

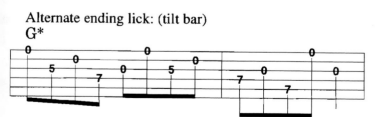

• Lesson 31 •
Roll Patterns
"She'll Be Coming Around the Mountain"

Roll patterns are often used to add drive and energy to a song. These patterns are commonly used to play bluegrass tunes on the resophonic guitar. *She'll Be Coming Around the Mountain* uses the *forward roll* as a primary roll throughout much of the following arrangement.

Definition: A roll pattern is a right-hand fingering (picking) pattern. The order or sequence in which the right-hand fingers follow one another when they pick the strings determines the name of each pattern. (See pg. 23.)

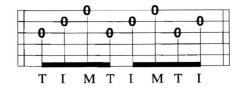

For Example: The *forward roll* = **T I M T I M T I**
(notice the fingering order or pattern.)

Each roll = one measure of tablature.

Each roll contains 8 eighth notes — not nine!

Each roll pattern can be played for any chord.

The notes should be evenly spaced — do not hold one note longer than another.

Accent or *emphasize the 1st, 4th, and 7th* notes in the forward roll. This helps to add a surge of energy to the song without actually changing the speed you are playing.

NOTES: _____

1.) Actually, this pattern can begin with any finger; the order that the fingers follow one another determines the specific pattern.

2.) At the end of the pattern, you can begin the same pattern again, or you can play a different pattern.
Do not stop between patterns—keep your rhythm smooth and steady.

3.) With experience, you will learn to recognize these patterns upon hearing them.

4.) Notice that *D Lick #6* occurs for the D chord (pg. 68). For practice substitute D Lick #1 for these measures.

She'll Be Coming Around the Mountain
— Using Roll Patterns and Licks —

Key of G

(quick)

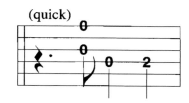

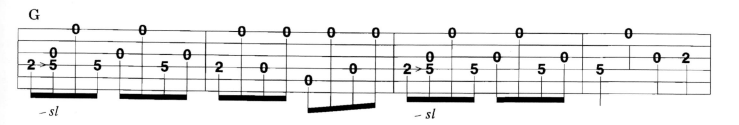

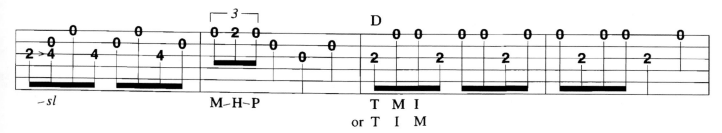

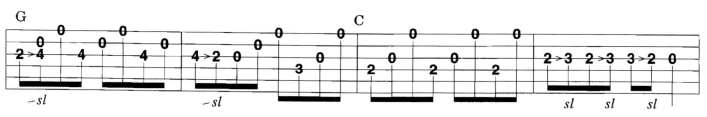

D lick #6

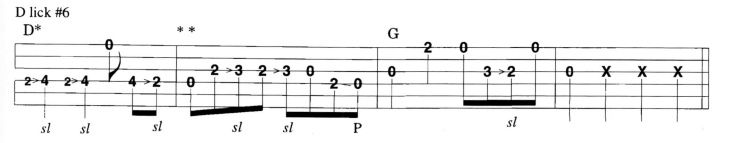

D * Substitute lick

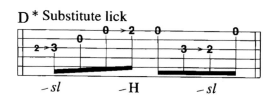

D ** Substitute lick - (D#4)

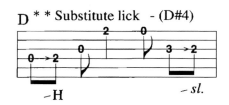

• Lesson 32 •
Rolls and Licks
"Lonesome Road Blues"

Lonesome Road Blues is a traditional bluegrass tune which has been recorded many times. Before you play through the arrangement, learn the chord progression. Notice that:

1.) The 1st measure is a variation of the *Foggy Mountain* lick which uses part of a *backward roll* (M I T).

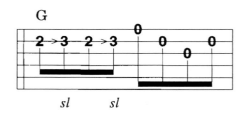

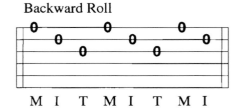

2.) The *C chord* employs the *forward roll* pattern, both times it is played.
   (Leave the 1st string open, but place the barre across all of the other 5 strings at the 5th fret.)

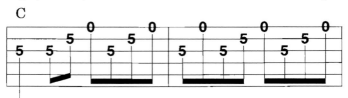

3.) Notice the *G lick* that follows the second C chord.

4.) **D Lick #7**:

   This arrangement uses a different *D Chord Lick* which can also be interchanged with the D licks on page 63 and page 68. (Notice that this lick also consists of 2 measures.)

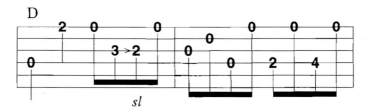

5.) **G Lick #12**:
   This lick is used as the final G lick. For practice, substitute other G licks in its place.

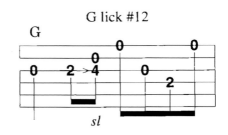

Lonesome Road Blues

Key of G

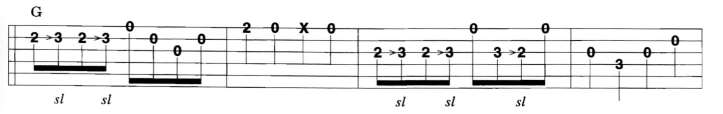

C lick #1

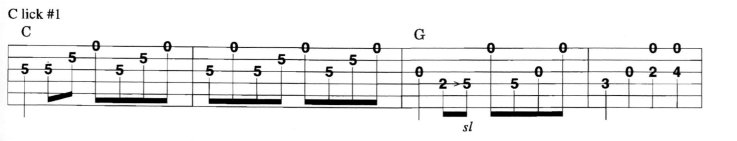

C lick #1

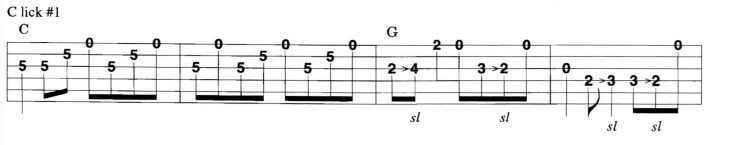

D lick #7   G lick #12

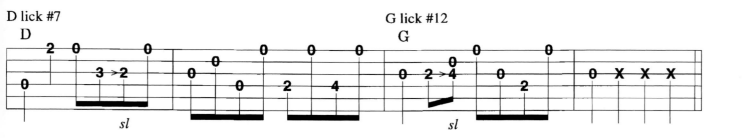

84

• Lesson 33 •
Roll Patterns and Licks
"Roll In My Sweet Baby's Arms"

The following arrangement for *Roll In My Sweet Baby's Arms* uses the identical chord progression used to play *She'll Be Coming Around the Mountain* (pg. 82). For fun, you can extract licks from one arrangement, and insert them in the other. For example, try switching the licks for the last D chord from one song to the other. This will help you become versatile at using these licks spontaneously in other songs.

Roll In My Sweet Baby's Arms is based upon the *Forward Roll Pattern*, with the right thumb picking the melody notes. The first D chord, in measures 7 & 8, continues to use the Forward Roll. However, the right Index and Middle fingers pick the *same string* each time they follow one another in the roll pattern. This produces a drone effect from the 1st string. It also emphasizes the D tone.

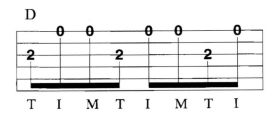

For the *C chord, C Lick #2* appears in the written tablature for this arrangement. However, you can also substitute *C Lick #1*, which uses the Forward Roll, if you prefer to continue the rolling effect through this chord.

C CHORD LICK #1
(Forward Roll)

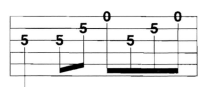

C CHORD LICK #2
(flat 7th)

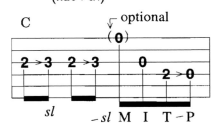

NOTES: _____
1.) Notice the driving effect created by using the Forward Roll Pattern.
2.) Remember: Two measures = two roll patterns.

Roll in My Sweet Baby's Arms
— Using Roll Patterns and Licks —

Key of G

↓ (short)

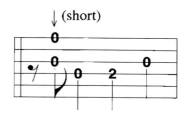

G Forward Roll

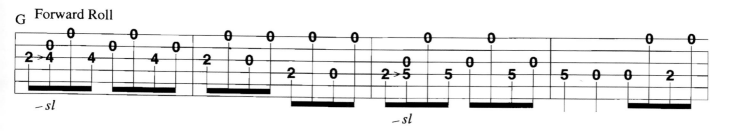

– sl   – sl

D

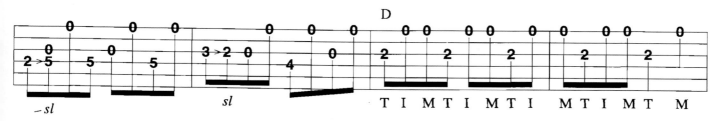

– sl   sl   T I M T I M T I   M T I M T   M

G   ** C Lick #2
C   (0)

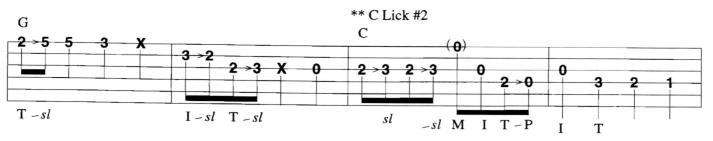

T – sl   I – sl T – sl   sl   – sl M   I   T – P   I   T

D Lick #1 pattern   D Lick #4
D*   *   Forward Roll
                                                   G (0)

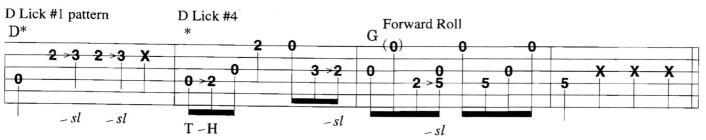

– sl   – sl   T – H   – sl   – sl

* *C Substitute lick

Play this pattern for one or
for both measures of the C chord.
(This is the Forward Roll Pattern.)

*Also: try substituting D Lick #1 (both measures)
for the last D chord. (See *Sunnyvale Breakdown*.)

• Lesson 34 •
The Choke
"John Hardy"

The following arrangement for *John Hardy* introduces a new left-hand technique called the "*choke*" (CH). This involves bending a string with the left ring finger.

To play
THE CHOKE:

 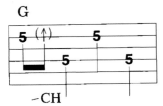

1.) Lay the steel bar across the 5th fret; cover all strings *except* the 1st string.

2.) Pick the 2nd string with the right middle (or index) finger;

3.) with the left ring finger behind the bar, pull the 2nd string toward you, bending *(choking)* the string in order to raise the pitch; (put pressure on the bar at the same time so the tone will ring). *Do not pick this tone.*

"John Hardy" also introduces a new 2-measure lick for the D chord. Although the D chord lasts for six full measures, it is actually comprised of three 2-measure licks. The final D lick (last two measures) is a combination of D Lick #6 (m. 1) and D Lick #4. Each of the 2-measure licks you have learned can be divided into single measures, and used separately. These can each be combined with other licks for the same chord, to form new licks.

D LICK #8:

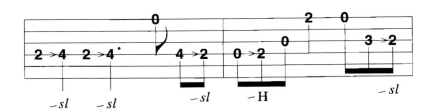

John Hardy

(↑) = CHOKE: Bend string with left ring finger to raise pitch [up 1 fret]

• Lesson 35 •
Improvising
"John Hardy"

The following arrangement for *John Hardy* consists primarily of licks. However, there should be no doubt in the mind of the listener that this is *John Hardy*. The chord progression, especially with the long D chord, is identifiable with *John Hardy*. Arrangements which are comprised of a lot of licks also work well as 2nd variations.

You can play this tune as it is written, of course, but you can also change it in many different ways. *This is how you learn to improvise,* and it is especially helpful when you are in a jam session and are called upon to play a song you don't know.

Music is much like poetry for it, too, is comprised of sentences. A *sentence in music* is called a *phrase.* Each phrase consists of *four measures.* You can easily learn to improvise if you can divide a song into phrases. If you want to include the melody in this tune, for example, return to a previous arrangement for *John Hardy*, extract the opening phrase (first 4 measures), and play it as the first phrase in the following arrangement. This forms another playable variation.

Often the 1st and 3rd phrases are alike. Look at the arrangement for *John Hardy*. Notice that the chord structure for the first three phrases is identical:

C	.		G
lick	lick	lick	lick

In fact, you can play the first phrase of the following version of *John Hardy*, three times in a row, then follow with the two D chord phrases (including the final G chord measures), and have a very effective break. The only difference among the first three phrases in this arrangement, is what is played for the G licks. Technically, you could play the same G lick in each phrase and have even another arrangement. Notice that the same lick pattern is played for the C chord in all three phrases:

C Lick #3*:

The *D chord* lasts for six full measures. This section combines three 2-measure "D" licks. Experiment by substituting "D licks" from other songs you have learned. For example, substitute D Lick #1 from *Sunnyvale Breakdown* for the last 2 measures of the D chord.

NOTES: _____

1.) The C Licks (for the C chord) are numbered in consecutive order, rather than separated according to whether they are "closed chord patterns" or "licks using open strings."

2.) *John Hardy* can be divided into five phrases of four-measures each.

89

John Hardy

Using Licks

Key of G
Capo on 2nd fret for Key of A

C Lick #3

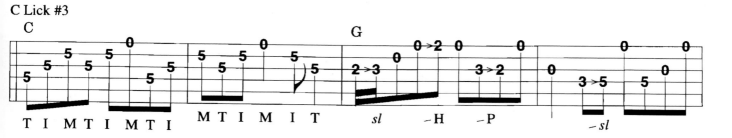

C Lick #3

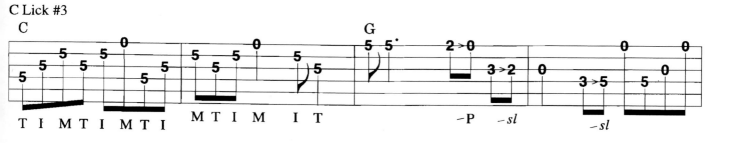

C Lick #3

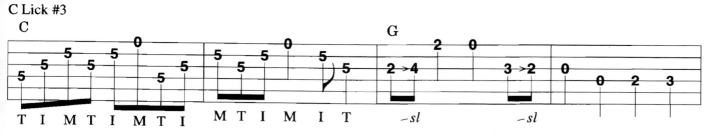

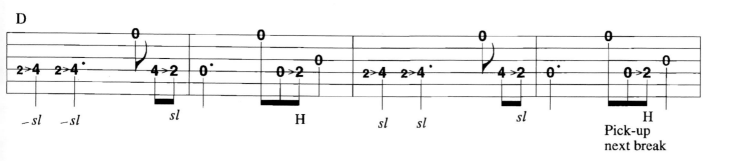

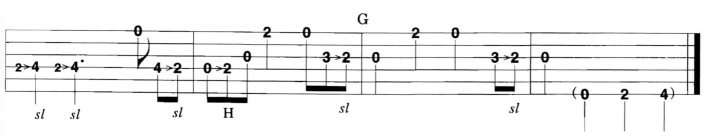

• Lesson 36 •
Combining Bar Techniques
"Sally Goodin'"

Sally Goodin' is a favorite tune of many resophonic guitar players. Each of the following arrangements builds upon the techniques used in the previous arrangements. This tune should give you a lot of practice for using the hammers and pull-offs and slides which we have introduced in other songs. These techniques will eventually become second nature. However, they may take some practice to play smoothly, at first. The pull-off, particularly, should be practiced by itself until you can play it cleanly, so that each note can be heard clearly.

Note: The steel bar should be tilted to play the individual notes throughout these variations.

This tune is written in the Key of G. The notes used to play this song, therefore, are drawn from the G major scale. The following exercise is one which will not only develop your playing technique, but will also sharpen your ear, and train your fingers to easily play in the Key of G.

1. THE G MAJOR SCALE: *Using left-hand techniques (hammers and slides).*

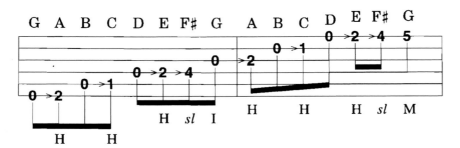

2. THE G MAJOR SCALE: *Consecutive notes played on different strings (melodic-style).*

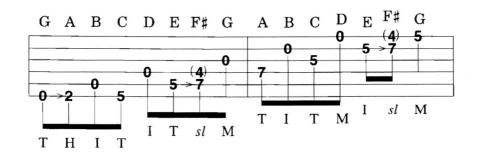

NOTES: _____

1.) We will cover scales in more depth in the melodic section in this book.

2.) The major scale consists of 7 different tones which can be played anywhere on the fingerboard.
It is called a scale when the notes are played in step-wise order. These notes are used to play songs.
The notes from the G scale are combined by composers to create songs in the "Key of G."
The chords we use for songs in the Key of G are also formed with these notes.

3.) The word "scala" means "ladder" in Latin.

4.) See *Footprints in the Snow* for the G lick, which demonstrates how the G scale #1, above, is used in a lick.

91

Sally Goodin'

Key of A
Capo 2nd fret

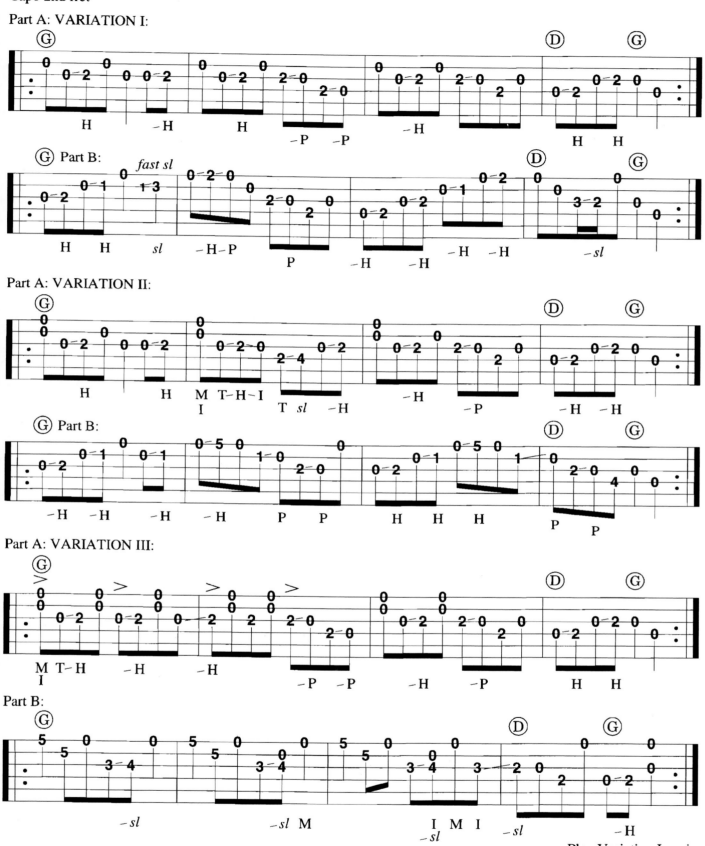

92

• Lesson 37 •
Review of Basic Techniques
"Fisher's Hornpipe"

Fisher's Hornpipe is another popular fiddle tune. Before playing this tune, study the tab for techniques you have already learned.

In measure 1:

Notice that it begins with a pull-off from the 5th fret to the open 1st string. Remember to *tilt or angle the steel* so that it touches only the 1st string at the 5th fret. Pick the string with the right middle finger. Next, pluck or *pull-off* of this string with the bar to sound the open note. (Do not pick the open string with your right hand.) (See *Cripple Creek*.)

Notice that the C chord in the first measure leaves the 1st string open. You have probably noticed that this is a common technique for the C chord.

Also, notice the fiddle-tune form: Play Part A twice;
then play Part B twice.

Look at the roll patterns played with the right hand for each measure. Part B uses the Backward Roll for the first three measures.

Do you recognize the lick in measure 4 of Part B?**

The next to the last G chord uses the melodic form of the G major scale (#2) in a descending run. Isolate this and practice it as a G lick.

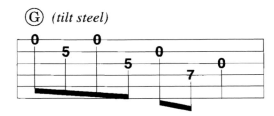

The final *D chord of Part B* uses a variation of the Forward - Reverse Roll which is also called the *Inside Roll**. Notice the right hand fingering. This pattern is similar to the closed chord C licks we have learned. To play this lick for the C chord, simply play the same fingerboard pattern with the steel bar across the 5th fret. This is a moveable pattern (closed chord lick).

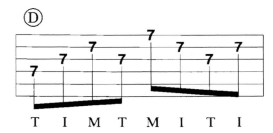

NOTE: _____
1.) This is called the *inside roll* because the right fingers pick the inside strings.
2.) It is a rhythmic variation of "closed chord lick #1."

Fisher's Hornpipe

D012

G Tuning - Key of G

Arranged by Janet Davis

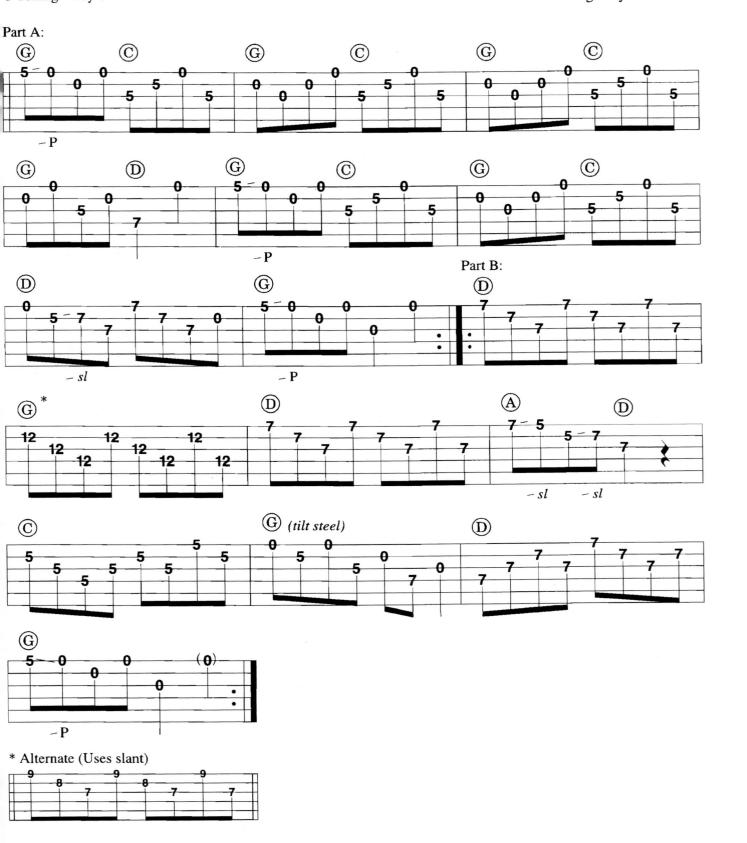

* Alternate (Uses slant)

• Lesson 38 •
Licks Using Scales
"Bill Cheatham"

In fiddle tunes, the melody notes often run along a scale line. When playing fiddle tunes on the resophonic guitar, it is common to play licks which are based upon scales. *"Based upon a scale"* means that the lick plays a *portion of the scale* either in ascending order (going up in pitch using hammers and slides) or in descending order (going from high to low in pitch using pull-offs and slides).

In a lick, some of the notes in the scale may be omitted. For example, in the G scale, the notes on the 4th fret are difficult to reach smoothly. Licks in the Key of G, will often use the following set of notes: (Tilt the steel bar.)

I.) G SCALE EXERCISE (This is the G major scale, omitting the 7th note {4th fret}.)

Notice that the Hammer is used to go up, and pull-offs are used to go back down the scale line.

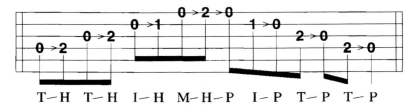

T–H T–H I–H M–H–P I–P T–P T–P

2.) G SCALE EXERCISE (using all six strings):

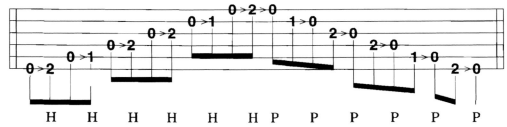

H   H   H   H   H   H P   P   P   P   P   P

In *Bill Cheatham*, the opening *G lick* uses the scale line. The rest of the song uses closed chord positions (except for the closing D lick). The first C chord uses a closed chord pattern which can be used in other songs for the C chord. It can also be used for any other chord from its own bar position. *Move bar back to open up the string as needed.

CLOSED CHORD PATTERN #5:
C Chord:

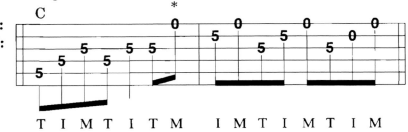

T I M T I T M   I M T I M T I M

* Move bar back to open up the string as needed.

CLOSED E CHORD Using Pattern #5:

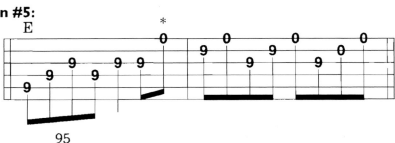

Bill Cheatham

Key of G

Part A:

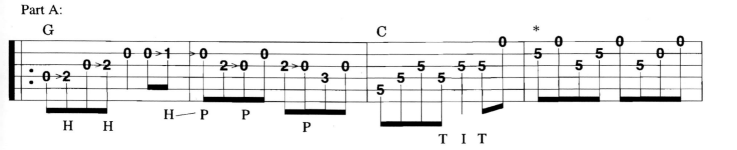

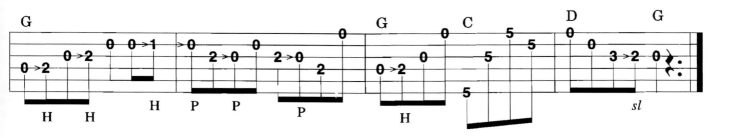

Part B:

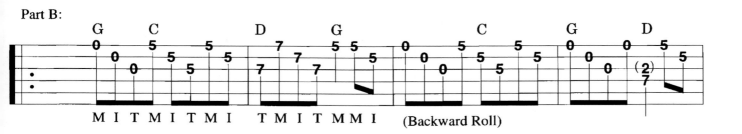

(Backward Roll)

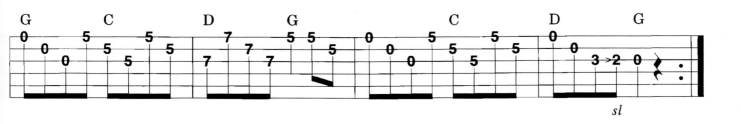

* Alternate

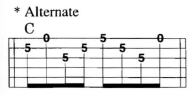

• Lesson 39 •
Melodic-Style
"Flop Eared Mule"

The following arrangement for *Flop Eared Mule* is played with a combination of closed chords and scales. Notice that the licks using scales are based upon the method demonstrated in example #2 used to play the G Major Scale on page 95. Instead of using the hammers and pull-offs with the bar, each note is played on a different string for the adjacent note. This is often referred to as playing in the "melodic" style. (Virtually every note is a melody note.)

Instead of
G Lick:

Play
G Lick:

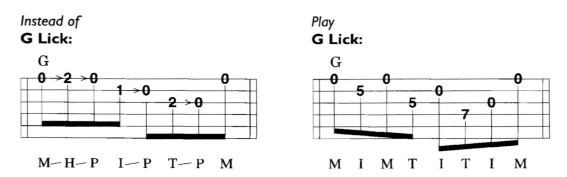

Refer to page 95 to compare the G scale with these licks.

A Chord Lick (Closed pattern):
(This uses the Forward-Reverse Roll Pattern.)

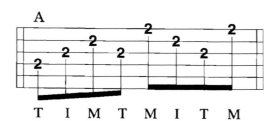

Flop Eared Mule

Key of G

Part A:

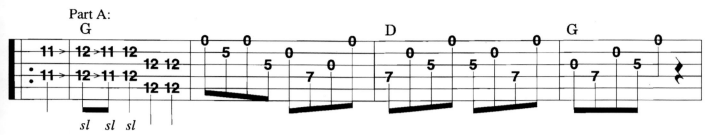

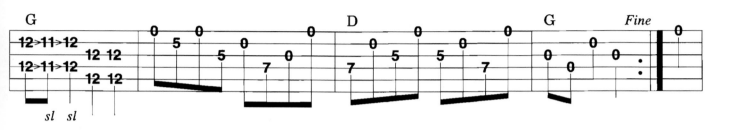

Part B:

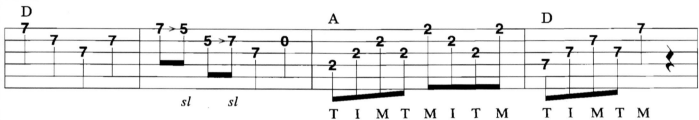

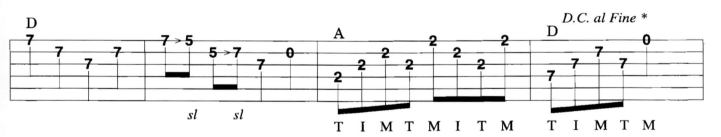

*D.C. al Fine
   Repeat Part A (only), and end.

ALTERNATE LICKS: (Substitute the following for the corresponding measures.)

D (for measure 3)

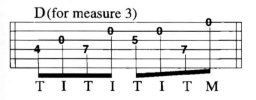

A (for Part B: meas. 3)

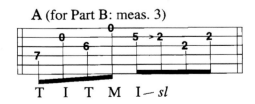

98

• Lesson 40 •
Single String Technique
"Devil's Dream"

Devil's Dream, another well known fiddle tune, involves picking the same string several times in a row, in a fairly *rapid* sequence. To accomplish this, alternate the right *Thumb and Index fingers* to pick the string. (You may use any two fingers that you prefer.) If you try to use the same finger to pick every note, you will find that it will slow you down, and the song will be difficult to play smoothly.

Look at each G chord in the following arrangement, and notice what is played:

    1.) In example 1, slide the bar from 5 to 4 to 5, without lifting it; you should also *pick each note* with the right hand.

    2.) Alternate the right Thumb & Index fingers in order to play faster.

    3.) Tilt the steel bar.

    4.) Dampen each string with the left ring finger, each time you lift the bar.

    5.) Place the steel precisely over the metal fret, not in between. (Check to see if you are doing this!)

Example 1:

Part A:

    T   I   T   I *etc...*

Example 2:

Part B:

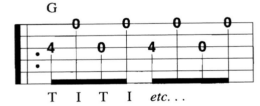

    T   I   T   I *etc...*

The last two measures of each phrase are played with the melodic style, as is the ending. The steel bar should be *tilted* throughout the entire arrangement.

Devil's Dream

Key of G
(Capo 2nd = Key of A)

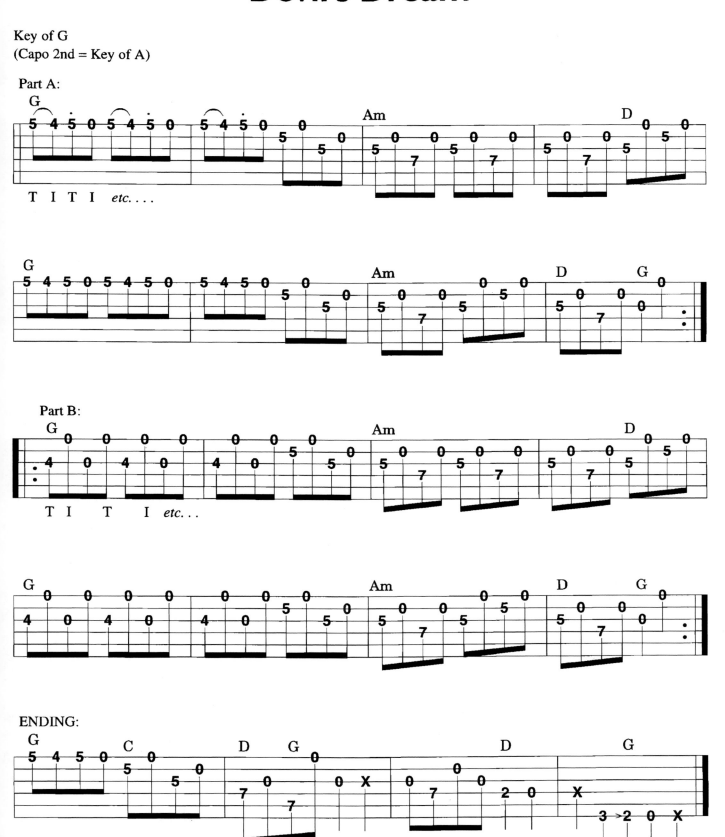

• Lesson 41 •
The F Chord — Melodic-style
"Red Haired Boy"

The following arrangement for *Red Haired Boy* is written in the Key of G. In addition to the usual G, C, and D chords, this tune also calls for the *F chord*. This chord lends a modal sound to the overall effect. You may notice this effect, also, in *Salt River,* pg. 80. Although the F chord is played at the 10th fret (barre chord), the following arrangement plays single notes on the deeper tones of the instrument, which are derived from the F scale. It is helpful to learn the frets which are used for the F chord in this area of the fingerboard:

The circled notes belong to the F chord:

F Scale:

The 3rd fret occurs in many F chord Licks.

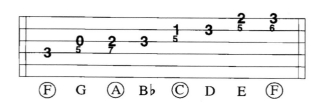

(F) G (A) Bb (C) D E (F)

F Lick:

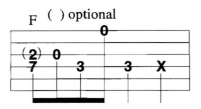

F ( ) optional

In order to be played along with fiddle and mandolin players, *Red Haired Boy* is usually played on the resophonic guitar with the capo on the 2nd fret, so that it is played in the Key of A.

NOTES: _____

1.) *Modal* refers to scales which were used before the 1700's as the basis of music. The G Mixolydian Mode uses the G chord and the F chord as primary chords (I and flat VII chords). Many songs from the Appalachian area have a strong modal influence. As they have been handed down through generations, musicians have tended to add the familiar primary chords (i.e. G, C, D) to these songs. Some people say this makes the song "feel" right.

Red Haired Boy

Key of G
Capo 2nd = Key of A

Part A:

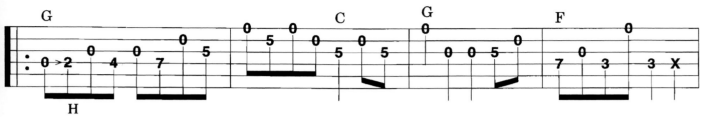

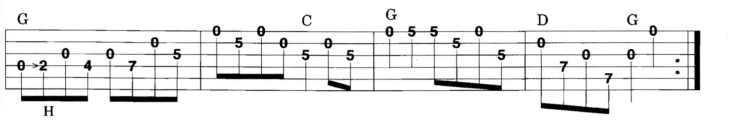

Part B:

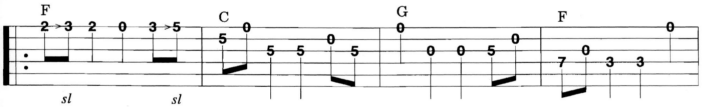

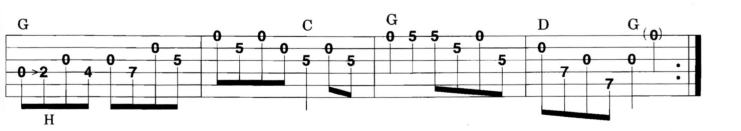

Play Part A twice; then play Part B twice.
* (0) = play only when repeating Part B.

102

• Lesson 42 •
The Modal Sound
"Old Joe Clark" — Melodic-Style

Old Joe Clark is another well-known traditional tune which has been passed down through many generations. Notice that this tune is also a mixolydian modal tune, like *Red Haired Boy* and *Salt Creek*. As you play more songs based upon the G & F chords, you will begin to hear a "sound" that is characteristic of modal tunes.

This tune is usually played with the capo on the 2nd fret. Songs which are "standards" among fiddle and mandolin players, (as I have mentioned previously), are often played in the Key of A. *Old Joe Clark* is also divided into *two parts: Part A*, which is played *twice*, and *Part B*, which is played *twice*. This form, called *binary form*, is very common among traditional fiddle tunes, as you may have noticed.

The following arrangement for *Old Joe Clark* is in the melodic-style, so that consecutive scale tones are played on different strings. When these tones do occur on the same string, a steel bar technique is often used. For example, the opening measure (#1) employs a *slide* from 5 -6. A *choke* can be substituted for the slide, if you prefer. (Fret the 5th fret, then *bend* the string with the steel bar to raise the pitch the equivalent of 1 fret, so that it sounds the tone which is at the 6th fret {F}.) Experiment to see which technique sounds and feels the best to you.

Using the Slide:

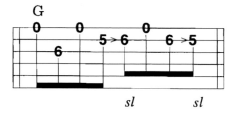

sl   *sl*

Using the Choke:

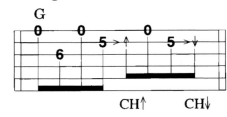

CH↑   CH↓

Note: 5 →↓

bend first, then pick, then straighten

Notice also, that the middle finger of the right hand picks the 2nd string in the next to the last measure of Part B. This is actually a *melodic-style lick* which is commonly played for the next to the last measure (G to D) in songs which are arranged in this style — using melodic scale lines.

Melodic-style lick:

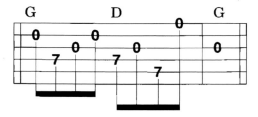

NOTES: _____

1.) See page 87 (*John Hardy*) for a more complete explanation for the choke.

Old Joe Clark

Copo 2
Key of A

Part A:

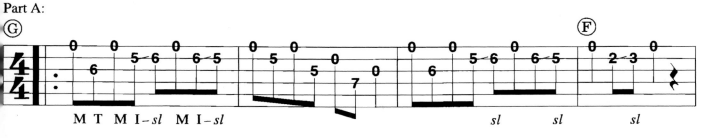

M T M I–sl   M I–sl   sl   sl   sl

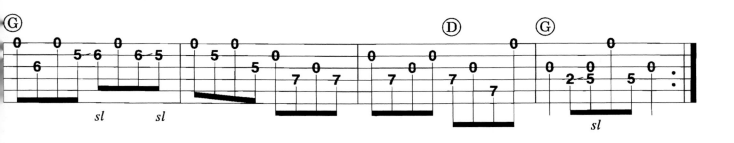

sl   sl

Part B:

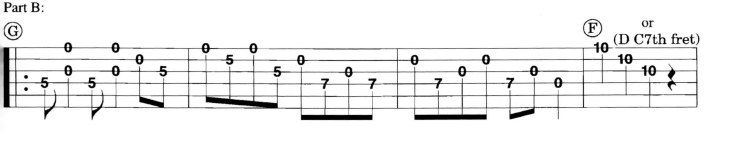

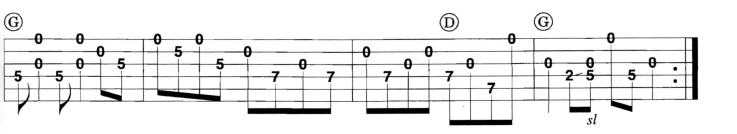

sl

• Lesson 43 •
Minor Chords
"Greensleeves"

In Lesson 2 (pg. 20), a chord chart demonstrates the fact that a major chord can be played across each fret of the resophonic guitar. These chords are played in alphabetical order as the bar is moved up the fingerboard.

A *minor chord* is simply the major chord with one note played 1 fret lower.

For example:

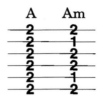 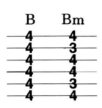 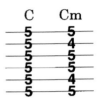 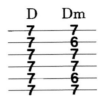

Obviously, it is not possible to note all six strings at the same time for a minor chord.

One way to play a minor chord is to position the steel across the fret for the major chord position, but pick only the notes which are compatible with the minor chord:

i.e. for **A minor,** play:

Forward Roll:

for **D minor,** play:

Forward Roll:

 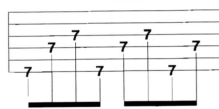

To play the minor chord from the "barred" position of the major chord, omit picking the 2nd and 5th strings with the right hand. (The A {major} chord is played across the 2nd fret; to play the A minor chord, *don't pick the 2nd & 5th strings.*)

In the following arrangement for *Greensleeves,* the melody notes are played as single notes throughout most of Part A. For the A minor chord at the end, the bar will fret the A major chord over the 2nd fret, but the right hand will omit the altered strings.

NOTES: _____

1.) Each major chord contains 3 different tones. These are derived from the 1st, 3rd and 5th notes of the major scale. Each minor chord flats (lowers by 1 fret) the 3rd; it uses the 1st, flat 3rd, and 5th notes of the same scale.

2.) Remember that the notes on the first three strings of the resophonic guitar are the same notes on the other three strings, but are sounded an octave apart in pitch.

3.) This arrangement is played in the Key of A minor, so it will not use the G, C, & D chords as the primary chords.

Greensleeves

EY OF A MINOR
andard G Tuning
/4 time

erse (part A:)

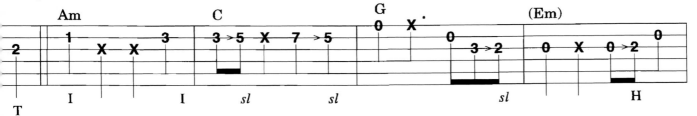

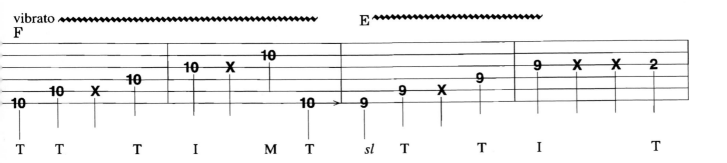

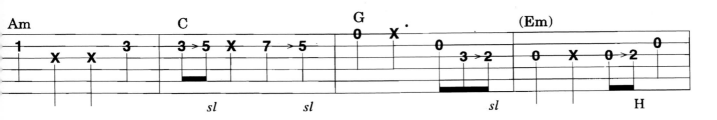

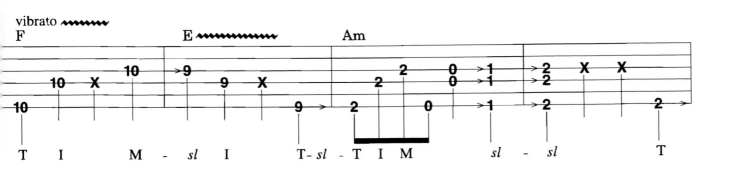

Greensleeves

cont.

Chorus: (Part B)

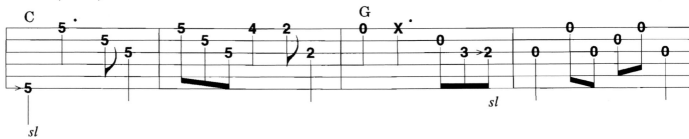

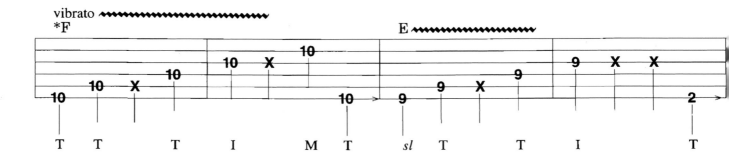

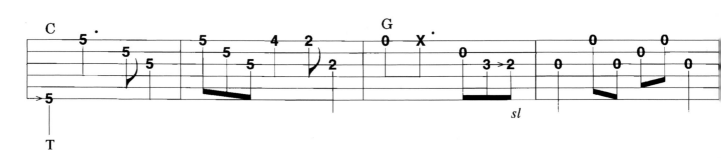

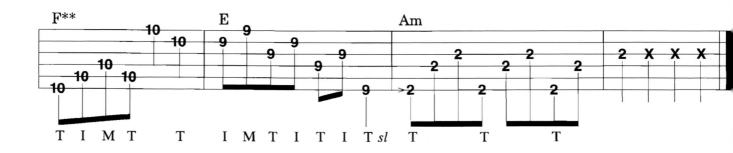

* Substitute Licks:
  The following may be substituted for the F chord and E chord (mm. 5-8) above.

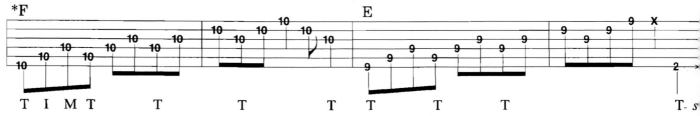

**The last line of the verse can be substituted for the last line of the chorus.

• Lesson 44 •
D minor
"The Battle of Jericho"

The home chord for the *Battle of Jericho* on the following page is the *D minor chord*. Notice that this chord begins and ends the arrangement; Dm also follows every other chord throughout. The D minor chord position can be played at the 7th fret, using the same fingerboard position we use to play the D major chord. D minor is the *parallel minor* chord of the D major chord, because they share the same letter name. Parallel minor and major chords (same letter name) can be played from the same bar position on the fingerboard. (This was also demonstrated in *Greensleeves*.)

Parallel Minor/Major:
(Look at the first measures of the arrangement on the following page.)

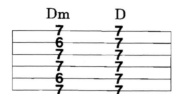 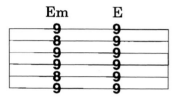 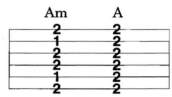

Omit 2nd & 5th strings of the parallel major

The major chord which is located *3 frets higher* than the minor chord position, also contains notes which belong to the minor chord. This minor-major relationship is referred to as the *relative minor* or *relative major chord*. D minor is the *relative minor* of the F chord (10th fret). The F chord is the relative major for D minor. The relative major chord is located 3 frets higher than its relative minor chord.

Relative Minor/Major:
(See measures 9 & 10 on the following page.)

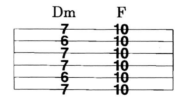 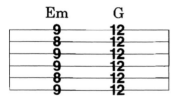 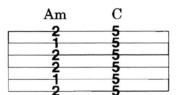

NOTE:_____

1.) The term "major" is implied. The F chord is the F "major" chord; D is D "major."

2.) The *Battle of Jericho* is another modal tune. The notes used to build all of the melody and the chords span from D E F G A B C D ... no sharps or flats. Although it has been contemporized with the V chord played as a major chord, it is played in the D Dorian Mode.

108

The Battle of Jericho

Key of D Minor
[Standard G Tuning]
[D Dorian]

Part A:

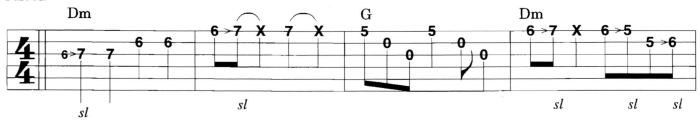

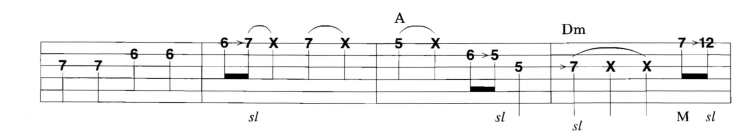

Part B:

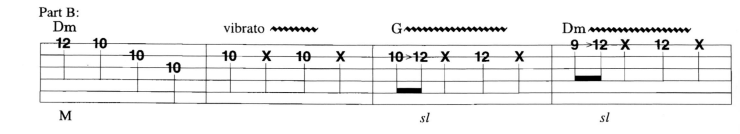

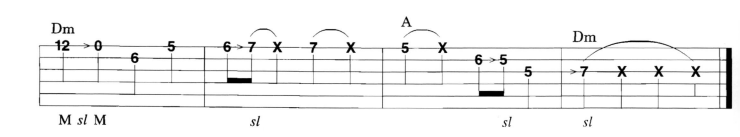

• Lesson 45 •
"A Minor" Blues
"House of the Rising Sun"

Another major chord also contains notes which belong to the minor chord. This major chord is located 4 frets lower on the fingerboard from the minor chord. To figure out the name of the chord, it is 3 letters in front of the minor chord letter in the alphabet: Am (G) F. i.e. for Am, play the F chord (A is at 14th fret; F is at the 10th.) Omit the 3rd and 6th strings of these major chords when playing the minor chord.

The minor chord tones can be played from the major chord position 4 frets lower.

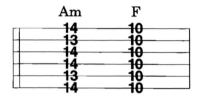 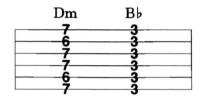 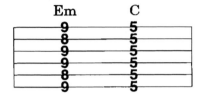

This should be played as a blues tune.

Summary:
The notes for a specific minor chord can found in the following major chords:
1.) Parallel Major (Chord of the same letter name)
    — omit the 2nd & 5th strings (this is the color tone of the chord {3rd}).
2.) Relative Major (located 3 frets higher on the fingerboard). (3 letters higher.)
    — omit the 1st and 4th strings, (although even these notes often work for the relative minor chord as the minor 7th.)
3.) Major chord located 4 frets lower on the fingerboard. (3 letters lower)
    — omit the 3rd and 6th strings.

NOTE: _____
  1.) These major chords each contain the root and the 5th of the related minor chord.

House of the Rising Sun

Key of A Minor
Standard G Tuning

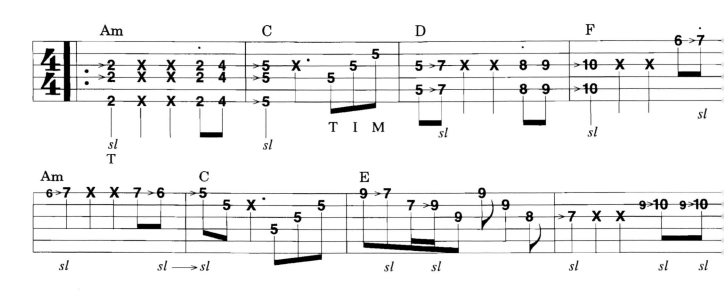

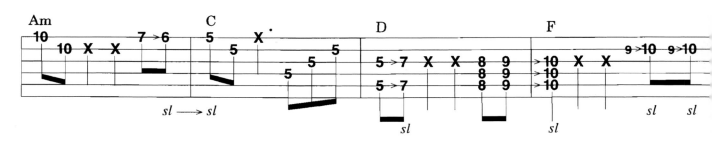

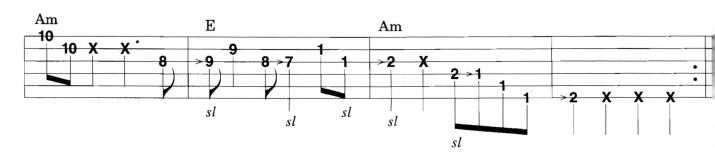

Staccato: = Quickly dampen the string with the left ring & pinky.
A dot over a note means to produce a sharp, QUICK tone.

• Lesson 46 •
Waltz Time
"Amazing Grace"

Before you begin playing through the following tune, notice that there are only three counts (e.g. 3 quarter notes) in each measure. Songs which are waltzes are played in 3/4 time, so there are only three beats per measure instead of the usual four beats.

When a song is played in 3/4 time, you should be able to say: ONE-Two-Three-ONE-Two-Three ... over and over with the music. The first note of each measure should be accented. Usually, this is a melody note.

For example: to pick the straight tune in 3/4 time, it would be counted as follows:
Remember to keep counting at an even pace.

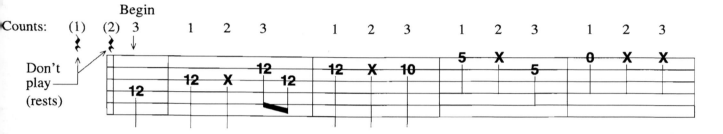

NOTE: _____

1.) If playing a roll pattern in 3/4 time, there will be only six notes in the roll, instead of the usual eight (eighth notes).

Amazing Grace
Waltz Time

Key of G

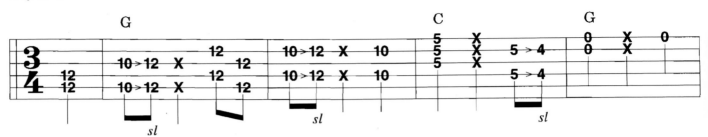

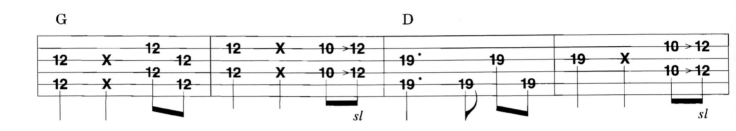

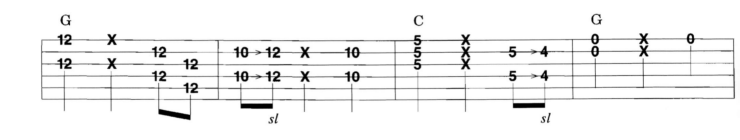

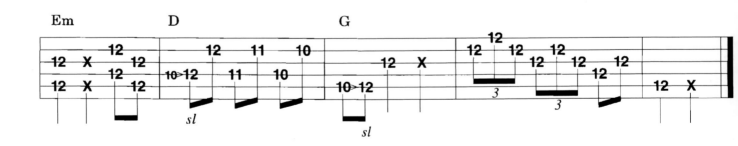

• Lesson 47 •
Tremolo: Waltz-Time
"Silent Night"

Have you ever realized that *Silent Night* is a waltz? The following arrangements are played in the Key of C. Therefore, the chords you will be playing are C, F, and G chords.

The first arrangement is fairly straightforward, playing the (singable) melody throughout. Notice that you will play a slant chord in the first measure with the bar.

The second arrangement embellishes upon the first arrangement. A fast Tremolo is played with the right hand by alternately picking chord tones with the thumb and index fingers. Notice that the Tremolo uses triplets (3 notes are played per beat). You can also double your timing by playing 6 notes per beat. (Remember to emphasize the first note of each triplet.)

 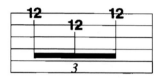 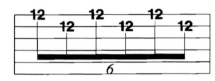

for 3 notes:

play 6 notes:

Silent Night

Variation I

Key of C
3/4 Time (Waltz)

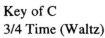
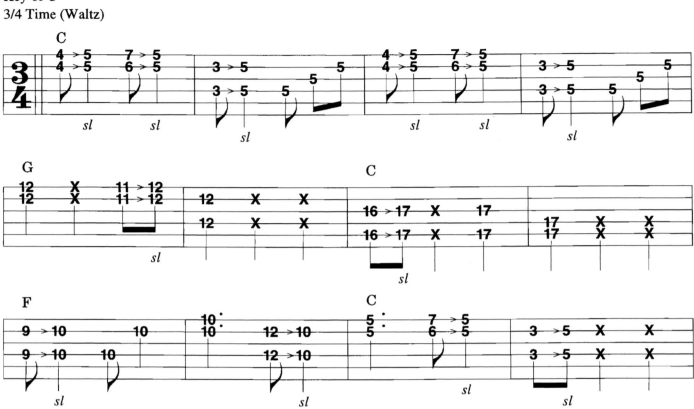
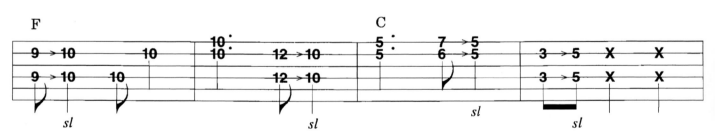
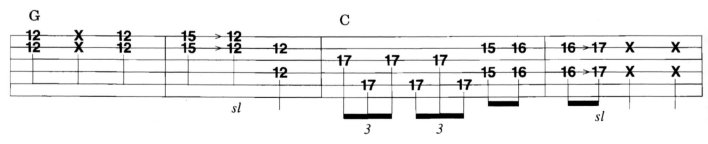
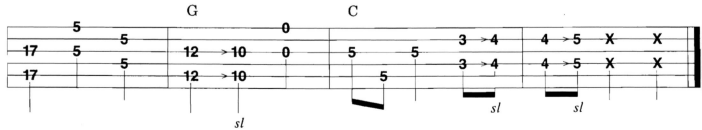

Silent Night

Variation 2

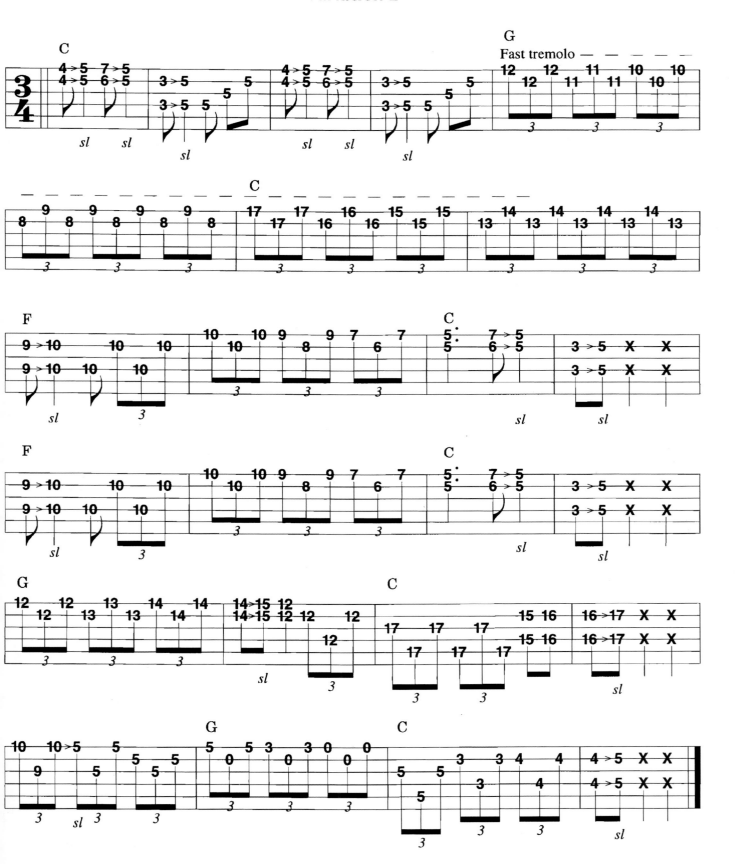

• Lesson 48 •
"In the Pines"
Waltz-Time Blues

The following arrangement is played from closed chord positions. Notice, the blues effect, from the flat 3rds (11th fret) and 7ths (e.g. 15th fret).

Key of G

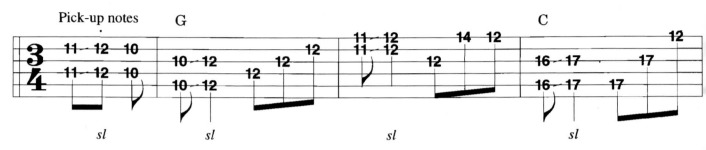

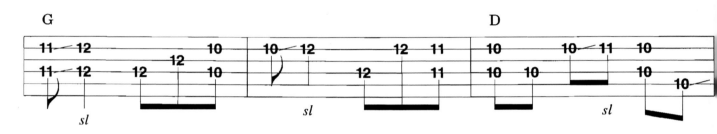

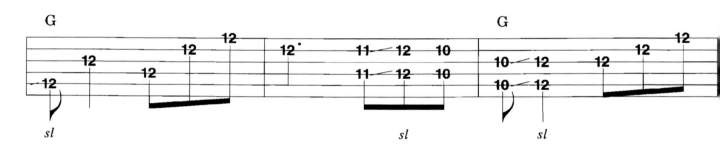

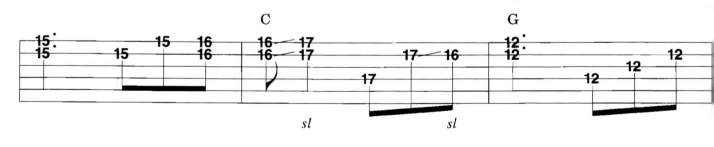

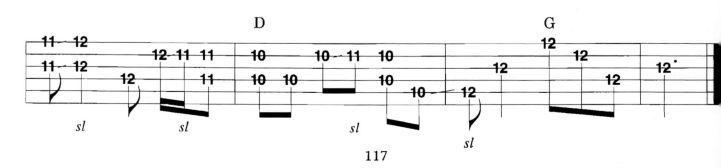

"In the Pines"
2nd Variation

Waltz-time (3/4 time)
(uses triplets)

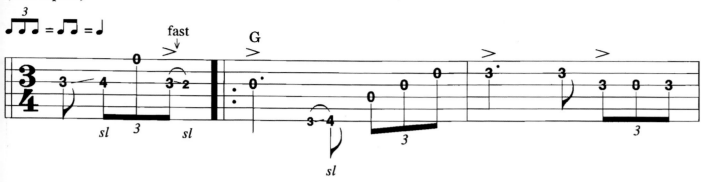

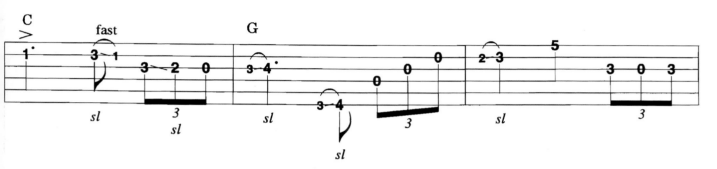

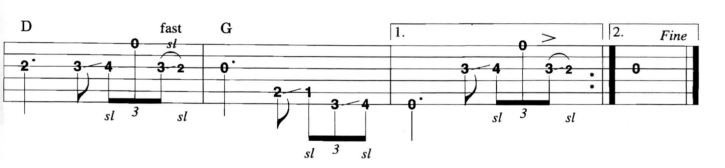

This arrangement is played by *tilting* the bar throughout the song. Notice the *triplets*. Emphasize the first note. The flat third (*blues note*) is played on the 3rd fret (3rd & 6th strings).

• Lesson 49 •
Slant Chords
"Sailing To Hawaii"

Although you can pick out most songs by using only barre position chords and single noting techniques, *slant chords* allow you to move *smoothly* from one chord to another, without lifting the steel bar. This technique is "dobroistic," for the resulting timber (tone quality) cannot easily be achieved without the slide effect. Slant chords are used throughout the following arrangement for *Sailing To Hawaii*. Notice how the slides which connect the chords enhance the Hawaiian effect of this tune.

In any song, when a double stop (two-note chord), is played on two *different* frets, it is necessary to slant, or angle the bar across each indicated fret, in order to pick both of the notes at the same time. When playing a slant chord, you will need to adjust (or lift) your left index finger so that the thumb & middle finger can angle the bar, without having to twist the wrist. The *wrist* should remain *straight!* The two ways to angle the bar are: 1.) with a *forward slant,* and 2.) with a *reverse slant.*

Notice that there are two common forward slant positions:
  1.) over adjacent strings (i.e 1st & 2nd strings);
  2.) over non-adjacent strings (i.e. 1st & 3rd strings);
      (Do not pick the in-between string.)

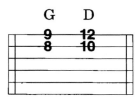

Forward Slant #1
(w/tip of index finger on steel)

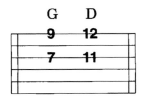

Forward Slant #2

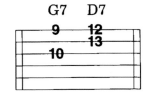

Reverse Slant

EXERCISE:

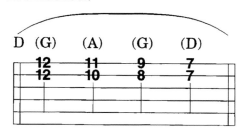

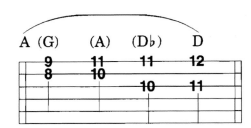

Place the bar so that it covers each fret of each string, exactly where the string crosses the metal fret. With your fingers controlling the bar, slide to each new double stop (chord); do not lift the bar from the strings when moving to each new position.

NOTES: _____

  1.) The Reverse Slant is not used as often as the Forward Slant.
  2.) See page 13 for more information on Slant Chords.
  3.) Some songs will call for three note slant chords, but double stops are more common.

Sailing To Hawaii
Key of D (D, G, A Chords)

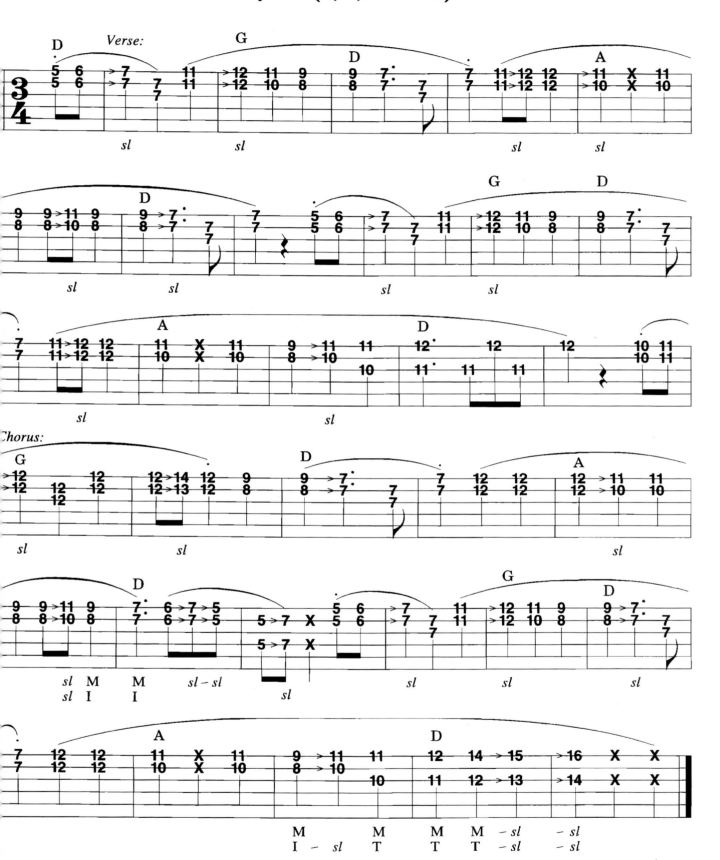

• Lesson 50 •
Adding the Blues, 4/4 Time
"When You and I Were Young, Maggie"

When You and I Were Young, Maggie is a popular traditional tune which has been recorded by numerous bands in a variety of musical genre. The following arrangement is played in 4/4 time, (so that each measure receives 4 beats). In the verse, a fairly straight rhythm is played, comprised mainly of quarter notes and eighth notes. In the chorus, the arrangement takes on a blues atmosphere. This is accomplished by playing flat 7ths and flat 3rds which we discussed in earlier lessons (see *Hamilton County* and *Reuben*). Another technique which is used to add a blues effect is to play:

Syncopated rhythmic combinations:

i.e. ♪ ♩   ♩. ♪   ♩ ♩
short - long; and **long-short;** along with notes of **equal duration.**

Also, notice the following techniques:

Tremolo:
Measures 7 & 8

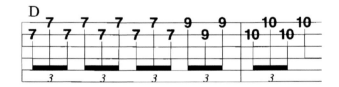

BRUSH: across all 6 strings with right thumb
Measure 14

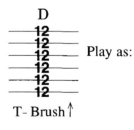

T- Brush ↑

(for D chord)

Play as:

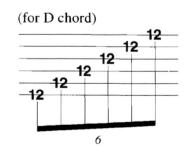

6

Reverse Slant:
Measure 15

```
G
                        8
        7 →9
         ▬
        – sl
```

121

When You and I Were Young, Maggie

Key of G

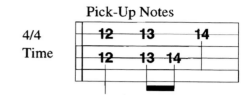

Verse:

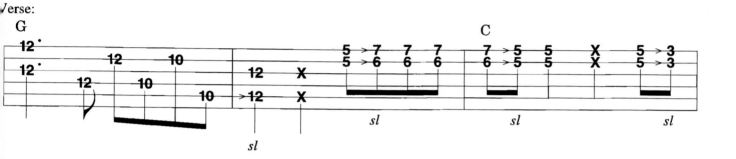

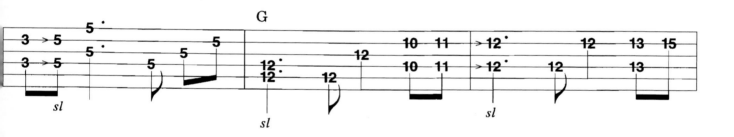

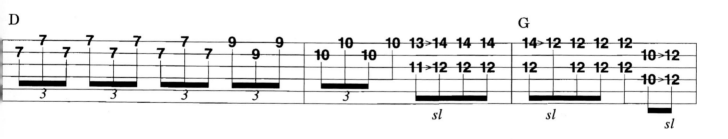

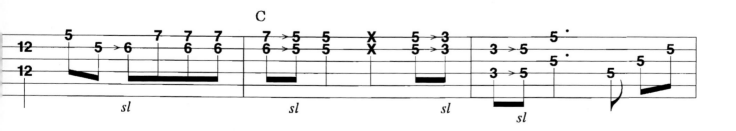

122

When You and I Were Young, Maggie

Continued

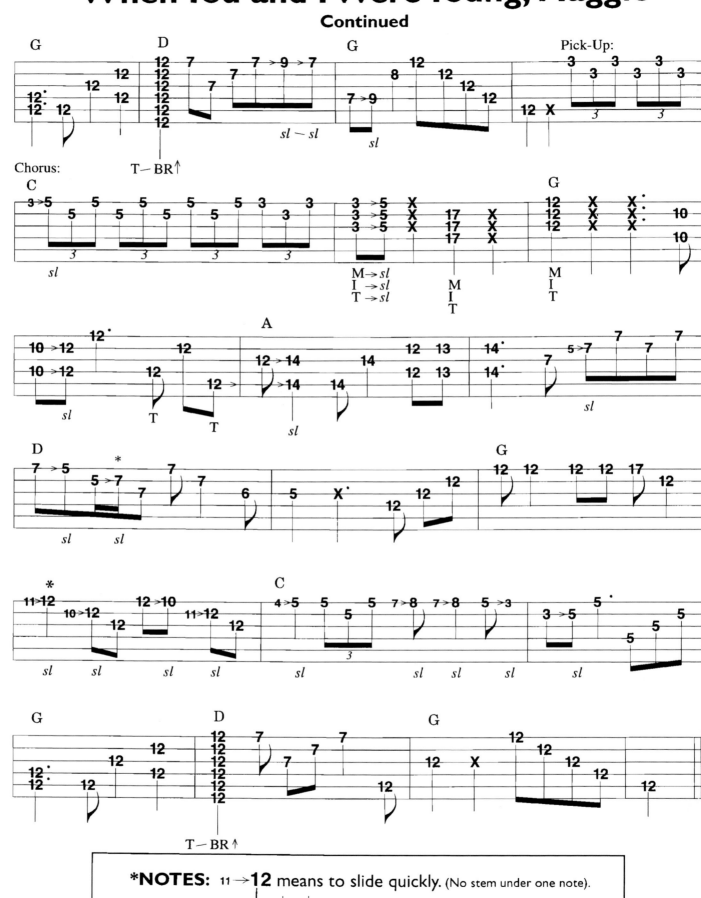

• Lesson 51 •
Slow Songs
"Silver Threads Among the Gold"

Many slow songs are played on the resophonic guitar using *closed chord positions*. Usually, the arrangement is effective if it includes the melody, or tune for the song, without too much ornamentation. In the following arrangement, notice that the embellishment is achieved primarily by filling in with tones belonging to the supporting chord. (Notice the triplets in the 2nd ending.)

The written arrangement for *Silver Threads Among the Gold* uses two types of musical shorthand with which you should already be familiar:

1.) *1st & 2nd endings:* play the first ending the first time you play the section. Then, repeat the section, but play the second ending, instead of the first one, the second time through. Then, continue with the next section (Part B).

2.) *D.C. al Fine:* (Da Capo al Fine) means to return to the beginning of the song, and play until you come to the word "fine" over one of the measures. This will be the end. Fine means finish. (The words, D.C. al Fine, appear over the last measures of the written arrangement.)

This arrangement also uses a backward slant chord, for the A chord.

Silver Threads Among the Gold

Key of G

Pick-Up notes:

4/4 Time

Part A: (Verse)

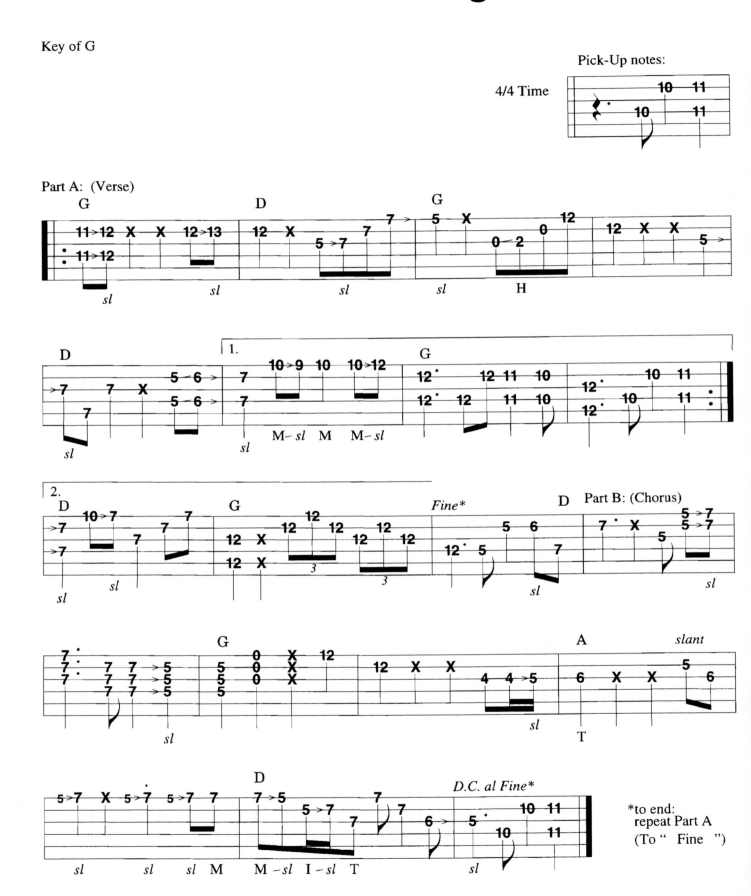

*to end:
 repeat Part A
 (To " Fine ")

• Lesson 52 •
Artificial Harmonics
"Dixie"

Artificial harmonics are chimes which are often used to produce a Hawaiian effect as well as a sweet or soulful sound. These are also used extensively in back-up, especially for slow songs. Artificial harmonics are more versatile than natural harmonics. All of the notes and/or chords on your resophonic guitar can be produced as artificial harmonics, whereas natural harmonics can only be produced only on certain frets. Also, the slide technique can be used with artificial harmonics, by sliding the steel bar immediately after picking the string. Artificial harmonics are indicated above the tablature by A.H.**** There are two ways to produce artificial harmonics:

1.) PALM HARMONICS: produced by touching the heel of the right hand to the strings, exactly 12 frets higher from the steel bar, then plucking the string(s) with the right thumb, and immediately releasing the right hand from the strings to allow the chimes to ring. This may take practice, but will be worth the effort. The heel of your right hand and your right thumb will strike the strings almost simultaneously. Lifting the right hand from the strings allows the chimes to ring.

2.) FINGER HARMONICS: If you only need to play the harmonics on one string, you can use your right ring finger or middle finger to stop, or note, the string 12 frets from the bar, instead of the side of your entire hand. Pick the string with your right thumb (under the ring finger), then release the ring finger to hear the chime.

FOR PRACTICE: place the heel of your right hand on the open strings, directly over the 12th fret (for the G chord); pick the 3rd string with your right thumb, and quickly lift your right hand, to hear the "G" chime. Next, place the steel bar across the 2nd fret to form the A chord; place your right palm on the strings 12 frets higher (at the 14th fret). Pick the 3rd string with your right thumb, and release your right hand, to sound the A. You can also pick several strings to sound a chord.

NOTE: It doesn't matter where the right thumb picks the string. The placement of the palm is what must be accurate. It is usually recommended to place the thumb a constant distance with relation to the heel of your hand, each time you play these harmonics, so that you can watch your thumb, yet your hand position will be in the right place automatically. This is the most common way to play artificial harmonics.

The following arrangement for "Dixie" uses artificial harmonics 12 frets above the each chord for every note in the arrangement. You can use either palm or finger harmonics, whichever is easier for you.

NOTES: _____

1.) Artificial harmonics can also be played like natural harmonics, if you use the steel bar as if it were the nut. In other words, you can place your palm 5 frets higher than the bar, 7 frets higher, etc. and produce harmonics.

2.) See Lesson 1G for more discussion and pictures for playing artificial harmonics.

Dixie

— Using Artificial Harmonics —

Key of G
Play every note with palm or
  finger artificial harmonics.
(Number over tablature note is where to place palm.)

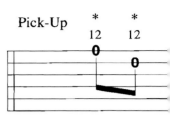

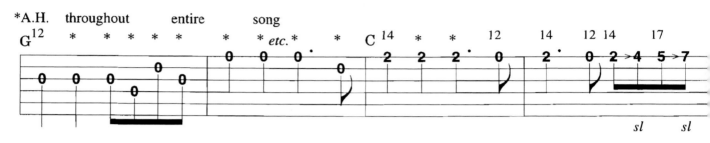

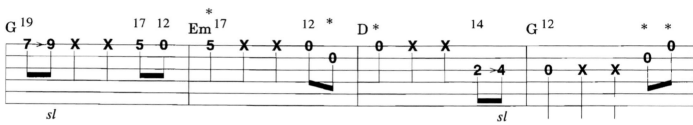

Chorus

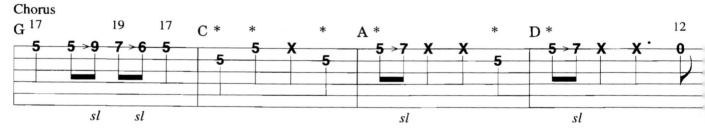

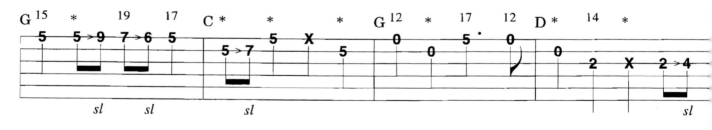

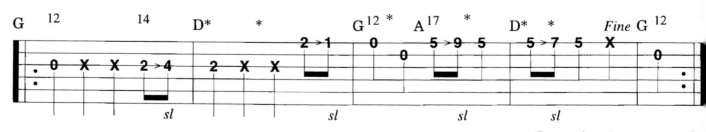

(Repeat last 4 measures only

127

• Lesson 53 •
Artificial Harmonics as Embellishment
"Aloha Oe"

Artificial harmonics are used to embellish *Aloha Oe* in Part B of the following arrangement. The right palm should touch the strings 12 frets above the A chord and the E chord to produce the harmonics in this section. The right thumb can pick the strings wherever it is comfortable. The palm location causes the harmonic effect. (Remember to lift the palm as soon as the thumb picks the string. (Either palm or finger harmonics can be used to produce these tones (indicated with *** over the tablature.)

This arrangement is played in the Key of A. Can you figure out which chords will be involved with this key, using the 1, 4, 5 formula?*

This arrangement uses many of the techniques we have discussed in this book. i.e.:

1.) The *tremolo* effect is played for the 1st ending of part A.

2.) *Slant chords* are used in part B.

3.) *Artificial Harmonics* are played in Part B.

4.) The *staccato* effect is used for the last line.
   The left ring and pinky fingers stop the tone from ringing. (Indicated with "." over the tablature.)

NOTES: _____

*1.) The primary chords in the Key of A are: A (I), D (IV), and E (V) chords.

Aloha Oe

Key of A (A, D, E chords)
(* = Artificial Harmonics)
$\frac{4}{4}$ Time

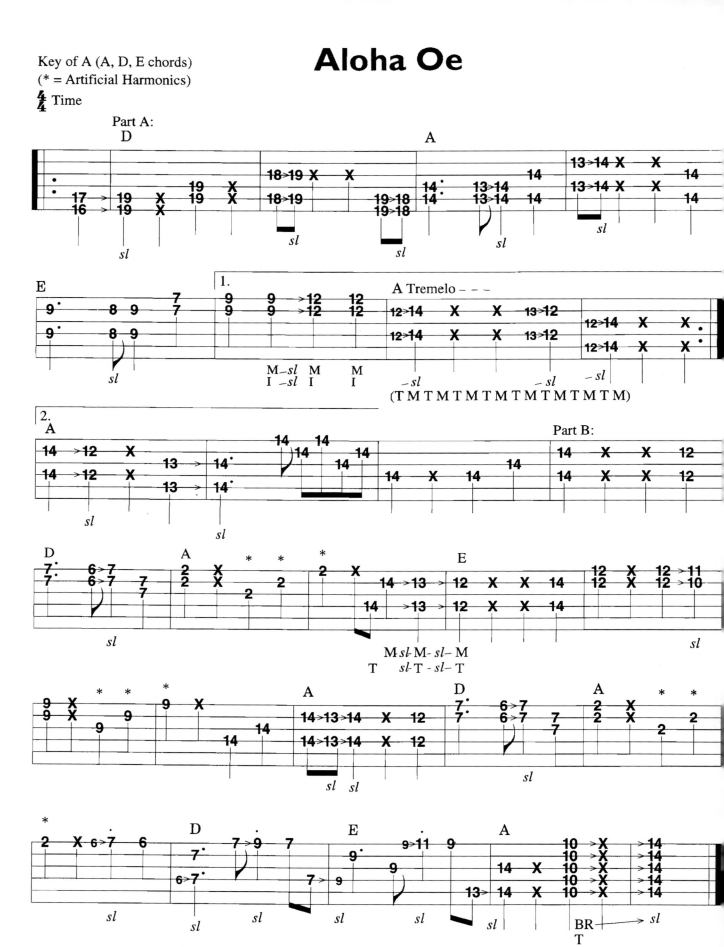

• Lesson 54 •
Transposing: Playing In Any Key
"Will There Be Any Stars?"

When a vocalist sings a song, the song is usually played in the key that best fits the vocal range of the singer. Therefore, it is often necessary to be able to play a song in any key the vocalist chooses. If you already know how to play the song in a specific key, then you will need to transpose the song to the new key. Transposing a song from one key to another is really fairly simple, and can become automatic with practice.

The first arrangement for *Will There Be Any Stars?* is played in the Key of C. To play this exact arrangement in the Key of D, you simply play every note two frets higher (in pitch). The distance between the C chord (5th fret) and the D chord (7th fret) is two frets. This same relationship applies when you move a song from the Key of C to the Key of D. This distance is applied to every note in the entire arrangement. In other words, to move a song from one key to another key, find the distance on the fretboard between the chords named for each key; then, move every note in the song this same number of frets. Notice that this tune does not use any open strings. This should make it easy for you to see how this principle works. The technique of moving a song from one key to another key is referred to in music as *transposing*.

Transposing from one key to another:

Key of C to Key of D:
What is the distance between the C chord (home chord for Key of C) and the D chord (home chord for the Key of D) on the fretboard? The distance between the C chord (5th fret) and the D chord (7th fret) is two frets. Therefore, to move the song from the Key of C to the Key of D, every note should be played two frets higher.

Key of C to Key of E:
This same relationship exists when you move a song from the Key of C to the Key of E. The C chord is @ the 5th fret; the E chord is @ the 9th fret. Therefore, to play this tune in the Key of E, move every note up 4 frets.

Key of C to Key of A:
To play the song in the Key of A, where would you transpose the notes?
C is at the 5th fret, A is @ the 2nd fret ... (5 - 2 = 3).
Play every note 3 frets lower in pitch to play this tune in the Key of A.

For fun, try transposing other tunes in this book. *Silent Night* and *Dark Hollow* would be fairly easy ones to try, since they do not involve open strings.

NOTES: _____

1.) Songs using open strings will move up in pitch the same distance as the rest of the song. If moving down in pitch, these notes will move over to the adjacent (deeper) string, using the scale line to find the distance.

Will There Be Any Stars?

— Key of C (C, F, G chords) —

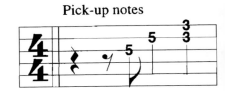

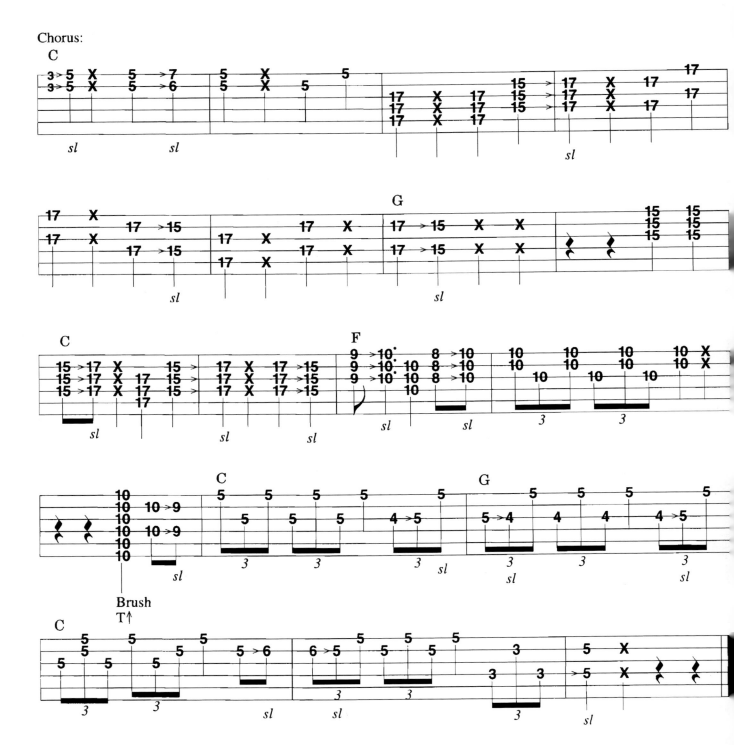

131

Will There Be Any Stars?
— Key of D (D, G, A chords) —

Moveable Chord Position Chart
Major Chords

*The number by each individual diagram tells you what fret the chord starts on.
*SLANT CHORD: Play any 2 strings in the position. These are played on 1st, 2nd, and 3rd strings **or** on 4th, 5th, and 6th strings.

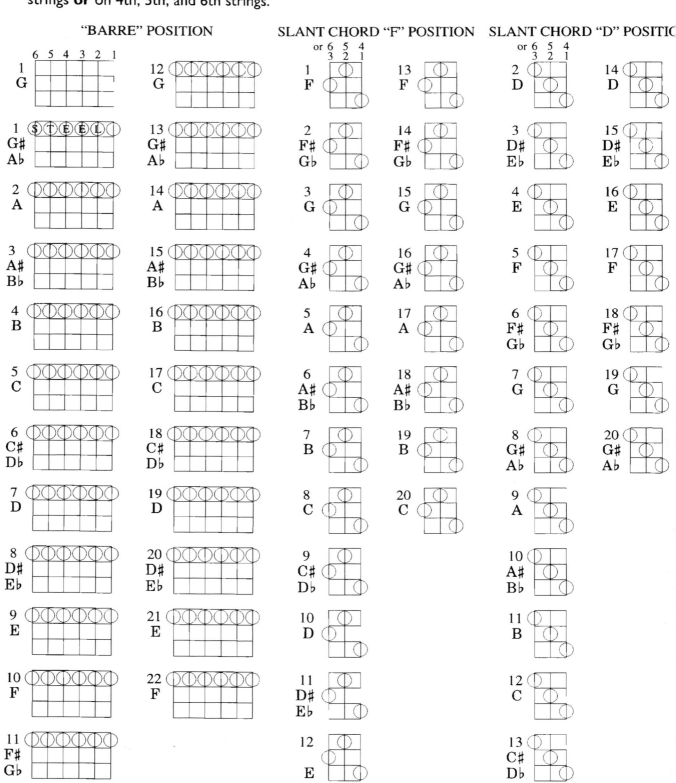

(The position is named for the chord in the first position.)